What others are say
A Faith Unleashed

A Faith Unleashed about a rescued puppy will challenge you to look at your everyday life in ways you never would have imagined. Joshua Masters words will touch your heart through the relationship with his rescued puppy Franklin. This book will hit home and hopefully be a guide for many people when and if they ever need a lifeline to know how to rescue themselves.

-Kevin Sizemore (actor/producer) *The Case for Christ*, Woodlawn, and *A Christmas Tree Miracle*

The first line of *A Faith Unleashed* deserves to be up with the great classic openers and the last line of the first chapter will cut your heart in two and mend it all back together with an amazing rush of Holy Spirit chills at how gracious, kind, and loving our Father is. In these 30 lessons, Masters moves you to a place of humble submission and awe of our God using illustrations and examples from a rescued black miniature poodle ... and now I need to go hug my dog.

–Bethany Jett, dog-mom to Sadie the Pomeranian and award-winning author of *Platinum Faith* and *They Call Me Mom*

In *A Faith Unleashed*, author Joshua Masters shares biblical truth through the unlikely stories of a rescued puppy. Even as we root for Franklin the pup, we find ourselves reminded of just how much God loves each of us. This book will warm your heart as it also leads you into a deeper relationship with our Heavenly Father—the One who rescued each of us.

–Edie Melson, award-winning author, and director of the Blue Ridge Mountains Christian Writers Conference

I fell in love with this book from its very first paragraph. Joshua has brilliantly woven the heartwarming story of his rescue poodle, Franklin, with a biblical approach to deepening our relationship with God, resulting in a beautiful book that will encourage you in your walk of faith. This is a must-read for those seeking a closer relationship with our Heavenly Father, those who love dogs, and those who have ever needed to be rescued, too.

–Michelle Medlock Adams, Award-winning & best-selling author of more than 90 books including her latest, *Platinum Faith*

You know how a pup who cocks his head sideways adorably forces an "awwww" right out of you? In *A Faith Unleashed*, Joshua Masters delivers the book version of a head-cocked pup. Heartwarming lessons of faith delivered through the eyes of a rescue dog. Oh my. You're going to want this one. So come. Sit. Stay. Read. Be challenged and inspired.

–Rhonda Rhea, award-winning humor columnist, TV personality, and author of 17 books

Author Joshua Masters has taken situations many of us go through and paralleled them with the life of his rescue pup, Franklin. By masterfully translating Franklin's lessons into words we can relate to, this book throws us biscuits of encouragement to see where God is walking us throughout our lives. Sometimes on a leash and sometimes not. Joshua gives us action points to rescue our faith where we may have gotten away from our Master and ran our own direction. What a great book to bring us back home.

–Tammy Karasek, Writer, Speaker, President ACFW UpstateSC, BRMCWC Social Media Coordinator and Reader Connections Coordinator

A Faith Unleashed

A FAITH UNLEASHED

Living in the Hope of God's Rescue

Joshua J. Masters

Bold Vision Books
PO Box 2011
Friendswood, Texas 77549

DEDICATION

Franklin the Pup wishes to dedicate this
book to the loving memory of his two
dear canine friends, Uncle Cole and Cousin
Moses. May their adventures with Franklin
inspire a new day in your journey of hope
and faith with Christ.

TABLE OF CONTENTS

ACKNOWLEDGMENTS

I'm continually grateful to God for all He is doing in my life, not only in the publication of this book but for His unending grace and mercy. He has lifted me out of the mud and mire of despair (Psalm 40:2) and allows me to be part of the work He's doing in the lives of others. As you'll see in the next few pages, He also brought Franklin the Pup into our lives with spectacular intervention.

From an earthly perspective, this book could not have happened without the love, support, and urging of my beautiful wife, Gina. It was she who first suggested my teaching illustrations about Franklin could be the foundation for a book on spiritual growth.

A heartfelt thanks to my parents, Patricia and Pastor Jay Dexter as well. They are true prayer warriors for me and have always been my greatest cheerleaders. I'm immensely grateful for your love, encouragement, and godly example.

Thanks also to Gina's parents, Ken and Madeleine Paquette, who are affectionately known as Franklin's Grammy and Pépère. Your support has been unyielding, and I appreciate you.

Similarly, I must thank my sister-in-law, Katie Paquette and Moments by Kate Photography for the smiling cover photo of Franklin. She has served as Franklin's official photographer for years, persuading him to look at the camera when no one else could, and dressing him in all manner of outfits from a chef's costume to pup-sized tuxedoes.

I'm also thankful for the author headshots provided by Jacob Calverley for this and other projects. He joins a multitude of co-workers at Brookwood Church who continually build me up and sharpen my walk with Christ. I couldn't possibly name them all, but my Brookwood family strengthens me as a pastor, writer, and follower of Jesus.

The members of my two in-person critique groups, Word Weavers Upstate and the Greenville Christian Writers Group, have been an amazing encouragement and have made me a better writer. That gratitude also extends to our greater online writing community and my fellow Blue Ridge Mountain Christian Writers Conference authors—especially Edie Melson, who invited me to my first critique group and Rhonda Rhea for introducing me to the Bold Vision Books family. Franklin and I are truly excited to be working with Karen and George Porter at BVB.

Finally, I hope the chapters that follow can provide a small glimpse into the love I have for that cuddly little dog named Franklin the Pup. He was an incredible help in the writing of this book. No one else would have been willing to lay across my keyboard, continually nudge my coffee to spill on my shirt, or beg to go out just as I was getting into a productive word flow. Nor would anyone else refuse to leave my side while I was sick, rest their head on my lap as they looked up at me with complete contentment, or bounce with excitement when I enter the house after a difficult day.

INTRODUCTION

My faith was chained—restricted and unmoving. I knew God existed, I even believed Jesus died for my sins. But deep down, I didn't believe He'd rescue me from the pain of this world—I didn't think I deserved rescue.

The crisis moment came as I walked the midnight streets of New York City without hope, carrying the belief I had nowhere to go. Feelings of neglect, rejection, and anxiety strangled me like a choke collar as I wandered Manhattan like a sick dog running from a puppy mill. I felt the urge to pray but was afraid God would reject me too. I'd run away from His purpose and calling on my life. Why would He want me now, damaged and ashamed?

But what I discovered, after a long journey of healing, was God had been pursuing my rescue the whole time. I thought a life of faith was the trap, but God didn't want to shackle me. He wanted to save me—not only in eternity, but now, in every aspect of this life. I'd lived with a shallow faith that only brought guilt, but God wanted me to experience the freedom of an unleashed faith.

I'm not alone. This struggle with confined faith permeates the modern church. When fleas or biting ticks infest a dog, he can become diseased. The pup no longer wants to eat, and his weakened legs give way to resigned fatigue. The infestations among believers are the unhealed wounds of our pasts and a quiet belief we must rescue ourselves.

Maybe you feel like an ever-tightening leash is tethering your faith. But God doesn't want your faith to feel restrictive. He wants you to experience a faith that gives you complete freedom and joy. He wants you to live in the hope and purpose of seeing yourself through His eyes instead of believing what the chains of this world say about you. How do we break away from the broken thought patterns we've been trained to believe about God, ourselves, and the world?

Enter the true story of a rescue dog named Franklin the Pup. As I allowed God to heal my wounds and reclaimed His call on my life to be a pastor, I worked in a ministry specifically designed to overcome the broken faith of those who are hurting called Celebrate Recovery. I'd often use illustrations from Franklin's life in my lessons because he too had experienced abuse, neglect, and suffering. He too needed to be rescued and loved if he was going to overcome the scars of his past. It was my wife, Gina, who first suggested these poodle-filled allegories of faith could be the inspiration for the book you're about to read.

I will offer one word of caution as you read. Despite the cute antics of an adorable dog and the spiritual lessons of hope in the pages that follow, these pup-parables are not perfect analogies for our relationship with God. There's a snare of the enemy in them we must avoid. It's vital as you're reading this book to understand God does not view you as a pet or a project. In A.W. Tozer's ministry with the Christian and Missionary Alliance, the pastor said:

> I heard a brilliant Canadian author being interviewed on the radio concerning world conditions, and he said: "I confess that our biggest mistake is the fond belief that we humans are special pets of Almighty God and that God has a special fondness for us as people." We have a good answer: man as he was originally created is God's beloved. Man in that sense is the beloved of the universe. God said, 'I have made man in My image, and man is to be above all other creatures.'

He's right. You're not a pet. Humanity is not an experiment or toy. We're designed in the image of God to live a life of joy, inheritance, and meaning as His children. But perhaps we can discover something about approaching God with the same loyal, obedient, unchanging love we experience from our tail-wagging friends. Maybe we can learn to depend on God's provision and unconditional love more fully by reflecting on the unwavering faith our pups place in us. What if we could lay down the melancholy perspective of Charlie Brown leaning on a brick wall and live with the continual, uninhibited joy of Snoopy dancing?

As you walk through the adventures of Franklin the Pup and his friends, I pray you'll allow God to speak to you. With each chapter, ask Him to show you what He wants to reveal about your life and relationship with Him. Make note of specific words or phrases that stand out to you and discuss what you sense God might be saying to you with someone you trust. Read the Bible passages at the end of each chapter and answer the questions in a journal, with your family, or in your small group. If you need encouragement or direction in a particular area of your faith, use the Index of Christian Themes and the provided Action Steps to an Unleashed Soul to help you grow and move forward.

As I write the final words of this introduction (and the book), Franklin the Pup has his body pressed against mine on the couch in our living room. I'd been working in our home office when Franklin walked into the room with his plush dragon and his big, black button eyes staring at me, a sign he wants someone to come sit with him.

I picked up my lap desk and moved to the sofa with his fuzzy blanket. Franklin trotted along, dragon in mouth, and jumped up onto our spot. Now he's resting soundly with his front paws crossed like a child pulling his blanket up tight, content just to be near to me. His dark curls are showing more signs of gray than he had at the beginning of this story, and he doesn't move as quickly up the stairs. But Franklin is happy. He's found a peace he never experienced in his past suffering. Soon he'll wake up for dinner and some playtime. His stub of a tail will wag with the unrestrained joy his peace now allows.

No matter where you are in your spiritual journey, my greatest prayer for this book is that you'll find the same perfect peace and rest leaning on the Father who adores you—that you'll discover a life of uncontainable joy as you experience His rescuing love. Only then will we live with a faith unleashed.

THE GOD WHO SEES ME

The first miracle of Franklin's life was that he lived. Born in an oppressive New England December, his first Christmas was anything but hopeful. Abused and neglected, the owners of a cruel puppy mill discarded the black miniature poodle when they deemed him unmarketable. He arrived at the shelter underweight, suffering from mange, ear infections, flea infestations, and a host of traumatic experiences we can only imagine. How could his pain go unnoticed for so many months?

Have you ever felt that way? When our own struggles feel unseen, our faith can lose its confidence. But we can only move toward unleashing hope in our lives when we realize God sees our circumstances. The soul is immortal. We carry our minds and personalities into eternity, but the physical world can wound our souls.

Sometimes, we experience the neglect and abandonment inflicted by this life and resign ourselves to an emotional cage. We shiver with fear, longing for a place to belong. Even when we feel we're successfully navigating our days, there's a whisper deep within our soul asking us to find a greater intimacy and purpose.

Whether it's crippling us or we're shoving it down in denial, the pain of our circumstances, both past and present, will distract us from the deeper relationship God is calling us to have with Him. God sees beyond what you show the world. He's working in your trials and will redeem the wounds of your past. When we believe we're no longer alone, we can confidently proclaim, "You are the God who sees me" (Genesis 16:13 NLT).

God saw the vicious way they treated Franklin.

He saw the impatience of my trust in Him.

He was about to restore us both.

My wife had large family dogs throughout her childhood, but I'd never had a dog growing up. This probably contributed to my obsessive desire for one. Two years into our marriage, Gina agreed I could start looking for a dog that would be a good fit for our family.

A search of four local and national rescue websites became an unhealthy, daily ritual. I acted with relentless focus, sending website links to Gina for dogs I had little attraction to just because they were available. I figured any dog today would be better than waiting for the right dog tomorrow. Gina rejected them all. She was willing to wait. Needless to say, as I studied for a life in vocational ministry, patience was not the first Christian discipline I developed.

I needed to learn how to trust God. I wanted to have results immediately, but He was preparing me during those months of waiting—arranging for the rescue of that small, neglected pup.

As my desperate search continued, the qualifications for finding the right dog became more stringent. We already knew we needed a hypoallergenic dog because of my allergies, but once Gina met our pastor's new poodle, Kodiak, she was smitten. Hypoallergenic was no longer specific enough. We needed a poodle—a miniature poodle. Years earlier, while engaged in a previous dog obsession, a friend insisted a poodle would be the perfect dog for me. I soured my face like I'd bitten into a bad lemon with a muddy rind.

"No one will see me walking a poodle," I said. Then I learned they didn't always come with that ridiculous haircut. So, I agreed with Gina, a poodle it would be. As the weeks went on, we had more discussions about the perfect dog and decided that we'd like a black dog and, if his character seemed to fit, we'd name him Franklin.

I continued my daily online investigation, but I needed to address a more serious qualification in my search. Gina and I were in tremendous debt but making efforts to change that. We'd dedicated our finances to God and committed ourselves to handling our money in a more biblical way. For the first time in our lives, we were using a monthly budget and climbing our way out of debt. There was room in the budget for the care of a small dog, but a large up-front adoption fee would definitely be taxing. Our price range maxed out at $200.

The task seemed impossible. I'd spent months unsuc-cessfully searching for a dog with relatively few restrictions without a single lead. Now I was trying to find a black min-iature poodle somewhere within driving distance for under $200?

There seemed little left to do but pray about it. I know there are bigger world issues to pray about, but seeking God is something I neglected to do when first embarking on this journey to fulfill my dream. God always sees me in my circumstances, but I seldom looked to see *Him* in them.

My daily search was taking a lot less time because none of the dogs met our requirements. The little black poodle I longed to name Franklin was nowhere to be found. There was always a moment of hope as the page was loading, followed by a frustrated sigh as a cursory glance revealed a list of dogs that needed a different family. It became mechanical. I was no longer paying attention to what I was seeing on the screen. I was only acting from a place of discouraged habit, but Gina knew God would bring the right dog at the right time and I'd somehow know it was the right fit. And so, I turned my attention away from disappointment and toward God.

Whether we're waiting for God to fulfill a deep desire or we're huddled alone waiting for rescue, the first step in having an unleashed soul and our faith renewed is to believe God sees us. He has compassion for what we're experiencing, and He can transform us through those trials.

Finally, one morning I staggered into our spare room that doubled as an office with a cup of coffee. I closed my eyes with the first sip as the computer fan broke the silence in our home. Trying to will myself awake, I entered the slow keystrokes I'd so often used to bring up the first website. Then, blurred to my still-adjusting eyes, a thumbnail image appeared on the bright screen, jolting me from my sluggish fog.

Is that a black poodle?

I set my coffee cup down and leaned in as I clicked on the image. He had a terrible haircut and was in rough shape, but there he was—a black miniature poodle at a small rescue shelter on the New Hampshire border. He was only two hours away. The adoption fee was $200, and the shelter had already named him Franklin.

Key Themes

Circumstances, Desire, Patience, Waiting

CHEW ON THIS: QUESTIONS FOR YOU AND YOUR PACK TO GNAW ON

Reflect on the phrases or concepts that stood out to you in this chapter.

1. Read Jeremiah 29:10-14. What does God's promise to Israel say about His character?

2. How can this be a comfort to you in times of waiting or struggle?

3. Share a time you tried to help God by implementing your own path rather than waiting for the good things He had planned for you.

4. How can you take actions of faith while still waiting on God?

2

WANTED

Have you ever felt unwanted?

Now that I'd finally found Franklin, I nearly broke the redial button on our phone trying to call Riverside Rescue. I shook my fingers loosely trying to relieve the cramp in my thumb. The years of remote control workouts should have prepared me for this, but I'd only practiced repetition, not intensity. I'd come across Franklin's listing much earlier than one could reasonably expect a business to answer their phone, but I was determined to be the first call that morning. A flutter of anticipation filled my chest cavity each time I pressed the little black button and moved the receiver up to my ear. I counted each ring, knowing every toll brought me a moment closer to the dreaded automated message that would taunt me with their regular business hours.

I'm afraid some poor soul who wanted a peaceful start to her day was sadly disappointed. As she tried to start the coffeepot, turn on the lights, and unlock the door, an incessantly ringing telephone undoubtedly jarred her from any morning serenity she might have enjoyed.

The world had abandoned Franklin, but his friends at Riverside were nursing him back to health. As he started the long process of overcoming the trauma in his young life, Franklin did not understand I was desperately searching for him. Even in the darkest hours of his neglect, I'd spent every day seeking his rescue. As the phone continued to ring that morning, Franklin was sitting in a shelter with neither a family nor home. Could he even be certain the workers would return? He was alone with his uncertainty and fear. Franklin's circumstances did not allow him to know someone not only wanted him, but was urgently reaching out for him.

Sometimes our relationship with God can feel the same way. Sometimes the circumstances of our lives lead us to wonder if anyone cares—if God knows the suffering the world has brought us. But while we're trapped in the perspective of pain, God is calling us. What if our sense of abandonment only comes from an inability to hear His call? When Jesus described God's desire to reach those who are lost, He shared this story:

> If a man has a hundred sheep and one of them gets lost, what will he do? Won't he leave the ninety-nine others in the wilderness and go to search for the one that is lost until he finds it? And when he has found it, he will joyfully carry it home on his shoulders. When he arrives, he will call together his friends and neighbors, saying, "Rejoice with me because I have found my lost sheep."

Luke 15:4-6 NLT

The man Jesus described in this parable is not looking for whatever random sheep he might come across. He's looking for a specific, individual sheep—one that he knows, one that he's desperate to bring home. His search isn't directed by a desire to have a hundred sheep. It's prompted by his love for the one that's in danger. The parable doesn't mention how he finds his little friend, but knowing how sheep respond to the voice of their shepherd, we can imagine he punctuated his desperate search with calls out into the wilderness as he listened for the faintest response from the one who was lost.

We can so easily feel insignificant as we settle into our cage of isolation. We try to find comfort in things no better than a tattered blanket in the back of a crate. We wearily accept our lot because we don't see any hope of change. Our environment and difficult pasts make us feel unwanted. They even deceive us into believing we're unworthy of saving. But all the while, God is unceasingly trying to reach us. He calls us again and again, waiting for us to answer. The noise of our chaos can shield us from hearing His voice, but He'll never stop hitting the redial button. He'll never stop calling out your name.

The shelter wasn't a home, but the people at Riverside Rescue showed Franklin the first real kindness he'd ever known. They saved his life, played with him, and prepared him for an even greater rescue of belonging. We might feel as if we've been left in a kennel without hope, but we may be in that place to help ensure our rescue. What if the people from the puppy mill had tossed Franklin on the side of the road and we'd never found him? What if he continued to endure abuse in a home without compassion or love? Franklin may not have understood his future from his place in the shelter, but it's exactly where he needed to be for me to find him. What if your next trial is just preparing you to hear God's call again?

Despite my less-than-courteous redial etiquette, the shelter did not hold my exuberance against me. There was someone else interested in adopting Franklin, but we knew he was meant for our family. I feverishly filled out the paperwork, and the organization began the process of making sure we were a safe and loving home for the little poodle. Within a few days, we were planning to pick up the young pup. As in the parable, it was time to rejoice with our friends and neighbors. Franklin was no longer lost, and he'd never feel unwanted again.

Just knowing you're wanted and sought after can transform the direction of your life.

Key Themes

Pain, Perspective, Self-Worth, To Be Wanted

CHEW ON THIS: QUESTIONS FOR YOU AND YOUR PACK TO GNAW ON

Reflect on the phrases or concepts that stood out to you in this chapter.

1. Read John 14:2-3. What does this say about Christ's desire to be with you?

2. Have there been times when the perspective of pain kept you from remembering God was seeking you? Describe how that felt.

3. How can knowing God constantly calls out to you change that perspective?

WHERE ARE WE GOING?

O nce you hear God's voice, the challenge can be trusting Him to take you where you need to go.

A week after we completed the paperwork, Franklin found himself in the back of our car heading toward his first real home. We'd placed him in a dog carrier with several blankets and a towel. He was just a little over four months old and still looked a bit rough around the edges. He'd been more than excited to meet us at the shelter but was nervous getting into the car. His legs looked unsteady in the carrier. He shook and whimpered despite my words of reassurance.

Perhaps he'd relax into the blankets once he got used to the crate and we started moving. At least the thought made me feel better.

We'd only driven about twenty miles of our two-hour journey before the horrid sound of retching began. But the rancid odor that filled the car quickly trumped the vocal distress. Franklin's nerves had gotten the better of him.

I pulled the car over on the side of a busy street, and we investigated. How was it possible for so much vomit to come out of one small dog? He couldn't possibly have any liquid left in him. The crate's contents couldn't stay in the car, so we cleaned Franklin up the best we could and threw the balled-up blankets and towel into the trunk. The carrier would need washing, but that would have to wait. As we scurried around the car, it was obvious Franklin was shaken. His body was quivering as his head darted back and forth, searching for an answer to his fear.

Once everything was as secure and clean as we could make it, we continued onward. We still had another ninety minutes of driving, and Gina didn't want Franklin to be alone. He'd just need a little comforting now, so she moved into the back seat to sit with the terrified pup as I continued driving. Surely this was a safe thing to do since he'd already expelled more than what seemed scientifically plausible. It turns out, however, he had plenty left. It was a perverse version of the loaves and fishes miracle. It was impossible for there to be more, but there it was. The next volley covered Gina. Her pants did not recover.

In truth, Franklin's anxiety was not unreasonable. Very few good things had happened in his life. He didn't know where this car was taking him or what would happen to him when we arrived. He hadn't known us long enough to build his trust, and there was no way for him to know we had his best interest at heart.

I've had similar reactions to the journey of life. We don't have control of where we're going. As much as we like to think we're driving the car, we're really not. It's become a cliché to say, "Jesus, take the wheel," but we seldom say that and mean it. Crisis events and past hurts cause us to have a warped sense of what we can trust and what we should fear. So we rely on our own ability to control our circumstances for our sense of safety. When that becomes impossible, our physical and emotional response is often anxiousness and uncertainty. But Scripture tells us we don't have to live with that anxiety:

> Do not be anxious about anything, but in every situation, by prayer and petition, with thanksgiving, present your requests to God. And the peace of God, which transcends all understanding, will guard your hearts and your minds in Christ Jesus.
>
> Philippians 4:6-7 NIV

Franklin has come a long way. He happily gets in and out of the car now, and he no longer gets sick when going for a ride. But that doesn't mean he never feels anxious. We don't have to wander too far from his known routes before he gets nervous and fills the car with high-pitched whining. He becomes overwhelmed with the "Where are we going?" question.

The reality is, we never really know where we're going. We make plans and predictions, but the future is unimpressed with our directives. Sometimes I find myself more focused on the road, its potholes, and uncertain corners than I am on God. That's where anxiety truly comes from. Turning our focus toward God is the best way to build trust in His ability to drive the car. As the psalmist wrote, "I keep my eyes always on the Lord. With him at my right hand, I will not be shaken" (Psalm 16:8 NIV).

If the Lord is on the right hand of the psalmist, they must be driving in England. But the point remains. Franklin's comfort in the car came gradually as he learned to trust us.

He needed to know we would keep him safe and eventually return home. God will often take us to new places we're not comfortable with, drawing us closer to Him as He further reveals our purpose and calling. Like Franklin though, my response is often filled with resistant whining. With each new path, I seem to question whether I can trust Him on this new journey. God is always trustworthy, but that only comforts us once we've experienced the peace that comes from trusting in Him. The transition from anxiety to faith comes from building a relationship with God through reading the Bible and spending time in prayer.

Do we constantly question where God is taking us or do we enjoy the ride, knowing His path is the safest one for us to take?

Key Themes

Anxiety, Faith, Fear, Stress, Trust

CHEW ON THIS: QUESTIONS FOR YOU AND YOUR PACK TO GNAW ON

Reflect on the phrases or concepts that stood out to you in this chapter.

1. Describe a particular time or event in your life when you felt powerless.

2. How would it change your daily life if you always trusted God to drive the car?

3. Read Matthew 6:25-34. What are some areas of your life affected by anxiety, and what steps can you take to turn those things over to God?

WHAT'S IN THE TRUNK?

Remember the vomit-laced bedding we put in the car's trunk on our way home? Franklin gave no thought to those towels once they were out of sight, but they still existed. We only hid the soiled fabric and its pungent odor to cope during a difficult journey. Once we arrived home, we had two very simple choices. We could either deal with the mess or never use the trunk again. The first option may seem like the obvious choice, but when it comes to the things we've hidden in our own lives, we often choose the latter.

Even now, Franklin's history influences his actions. Every anxiety or behavioral issue stems from the circumstances and lessons of his past. Another dog wouldn't even look up from his plush hedgehog if someone wiped their shoes on the mat or swept fuzz off an ottoman, but Franklin despises it.

His fear and anger often swell into a panicked tantrum, and it's one of the few circumstances when he might nip at someone's leg. Did the person who abused Franklin have a habit of wiping their feet? Does the motion remind him of being kicked or hit? We don't know, but something from his time in the puppy mill causes him to react with violent defense when he hears someone's feet scraping against a mat. Over time, his reaction has lessened, but there's still something awful hidden in the trunk of his life.

We are incapable of looking at our own behavior objectively because we see things through the warped lens of our broken past. We accept the lies the world's taught us about ourselves and believe the lies of our own making. There's something about a man wiping his feet that triggers a reaction of fear in Franklin. It's not based on the truth of his current circumstances, but he believes he isn't safe.

There are things in our past that make us believe similar falsehoods. Perhaps the way your father treated you planted the lie that you're worthless. Maybe the betrayal of a spouse has convinced you you're unlovable. A history of abuse can cause the false belief that you're irreparably damaged or expendable. Maybe you struggle with anger or control issues and don't know why it's triggered so often in your life. Whatever the struggle, the things we believe about ourselves, the world, and God determine both our internal and external response to everything. We try to ignore the soiled remnants of pain and fear we've tucked away in the trunk of our personal lives because we're afraid of what we might find when we open it. And because we haven't dealt with the mess, it continues to distract us from making healthy decisions.

I've already mentioned I was in a great deal of debt before I married Gina or adopted Franklin. I had no interest in discussing my finances with God or anyone who had sound advice. I couldn't pay my bills, and I was so afraid to open the envelopes in my mailbox stamped, "OPEN

IMMEDIATELY." I tossed them in a pile, and when the stack of bills taunted me, I'd throw it in a plastic grocery bag and hide it in the basement stairwell.

"I'll go through all those bags this weekend," I'd say. Then I'd go to the store and buy some DVDs with a credit card to make myself feel better. I never opened that door except to add another bag of ignored consequences to the pile. Consider this fitting proverb: "As a dog returns to its vomit, so a fool repeats his foolishness" (Proverbs 26:11 NLT).

As long as we refuse to clean up the vomit in our own hiding place, we'll continue to revisit it with unhealthy behaviors. You can push it deep into an emotional closet and make excuses not to look in its direction—even convincing yourself for a moment the mess isn't there—but it will affect every choice you make until you've addressed the root issue behind the behavior.

Franklin's fear of feet dragging across a rug is irrational, but it's based on the experiences of his past. He hasn't lived in the promise of a greater truth that contradicts the lie governing his actions. The only way to correct that is for him to experience the safety we provide as we retrain him to see the world as it is under our protection.

God doesn't want you trapped in the lies of past hurts. He wants you set free in the safety of His promises. He has a greater purpose for your life than the misrepresented details of your past will allow. To move forward, we must examine the past, seek God's truth about it, and leave it behind. Paul took part in killing Christians before Jesus transformed him. He knew the pain of sin and regret, but he told the Philippians,

No, dear brothers and sisters, I have not achieved it [perfection], but I focus on this one thing: Forgetting the past and looking forward to what lies ahead, I press on to reach the end of the race and receive the heavenly prize for which God, through Christ Jesus, is calling us.

Philippians 3:13-14 NLT

Paul knew he could only fulfill the mission God had for his life if he cleaned out all the shame and baggage he could have continued to carry. God changed the world through Paul's ministry. It wasn't because Paul was great, but because he exposed the stains of his past so they could be cleaned. Paul wrote portions of the New Testament, encouraged other believers, and trained churches all while physically chained in a prison. He only had the strength to do that because he allowed God to remove the shackles on his soul. If we want to experience the new life God has for us, we must become willing to do the same.

To revisit the original conundrum of our story, we chose to clean the trunk rather than buy a new car.

Key Themes

Decisions, Fear, Pain, Your Past

CHEW ON THIS: QUESTIONS FOR YOU AND YOUR PACK TO GNAW ON

Reflect on the phrases or concepts that stood out to you in this chapter.

1. Ask God to reveal the issues from your past that need to be addressed and what false perspectives are affecting your behavior. What is He bringing to mind?

2. What is the difference between leaving your past behind and ignoring the past?

3. Read Philippians 3:8-14. What steps can you take in leaving your past behind?

A NEW LIFE

To experience an unleashed soul, we must go beyond the healing of our old life and embrace the blessings of the new one.

With the adoption complete, a perilous journey behind us, and a sparkling car trunk, it was time for the young pup to start a new life—one he didn't know how to live. His old life of neglect was becoming his history instead of his identity. Franklin experienced a difficult existence with continual fear before joining our family. From moment to moment, he never knew if someone would love him or bring further abuse. Each person who approached him could represent kindness or cruelty. He had a clear affection for the people who'd rescued him at the shelter, but his future remained so uncertain. Was sleeping on a donated kennel blanket the best life he could expect or was there something more?

When we face those kinds of struggles, the enemy of our soul manipulates us into believing our circumstances are the mirror of our identity. Convincing us the two are only a reflection of one another is the easiest way to ensure we surrender our hope for a better future. If Satan can't use our past against us, he'll make us question the future, using the chaos of this life to distract us from God's promise of a greater one. Jesus said, "The thief's purpose is to steal and kill and destroy. My purpose is to give them a rich and satisfying life" (John 10:10 NLT). But if the trials of a fractured world are the measure of our value, there's little reason to expect any change in our lives. If I believe I *am* my broken circumstances, I'll always see myself as broken and unworthy.

We do not establish the value of a puppy by his treatment in a puppy mill. Any reasonable person knows a puppy is worthy of protection from evil because his value isn't determined by his circumstances. His value is inherent. And so is yours. Why then do we allow our current situations to prevent us from claiming the new life being offered to us?

Gina and I were giving Franklin a new life, but he was tentative. To him, entering our home just felt like the next place he was being taken. He moved slowly at first, unsure of his surroundings. His closely shaved snout pushed along the edge of the entryway, and his wildly unkempt puppy hair rocked back and forth as he ambled down the short hallway. Poodles have hair rather than fur, so it had the airy texture of a baby's first locks. We were already falling in love with him, but his amusing movements and dancing curls were only a cover for a deep discomfort with this new environment. I picked up a broom to move it out of his way, and he cowered. Gina made a sound, and he jumped anxiously with a startled turn toward the noise. It would take time for him to trust us.

He gratefully accepted our hugs and gentle pets, but his experiences as a defenseless pup had trained him to believe he was never safe. Even though his past was now behind him, he'd never lived an existence of love, protection, and provision. So he couldn't understand the good things we had prepared for him. Franklin's uncertainty trapped him between the life he was leaving and the potential of his new path with us.

Sometimes our fear and low expectations obscure the difficult journey toward something better God has in store. In reality, He's preparing a transformed life for us just as He promised His people in the book of Isaiah:

> For I am about to do something new. See, I have already begun! Do you not see it? I will make a pathway through the wilderness. I will create rivers in the dry wasteland. The wild animals in the fields will thank me, the jackals and owls, too, for giving them water in the desert. Yes, I will make rivers in the dry wasteland So my chosen people can be refreshed.
>
> Isaiah 43:19-20 NLT

Franklin's days are filled with naps in the sun room, playtime in the evening, and a dedicated place at the foot of our king-sized bed now. He has a fenced-in yard where he runs and plays fetch. He eats quality food and spends a good amount of time in someone's lap. He looks to us when he's hungry or needs to go out. He's learned to live in complete reliance on us without fear of neglect or abuse.

It has transformed everything about his life, but none of that was in focus for him on the day he arrived. In the passage above, God had already begun a new work and questions why His people couldn't see it. Perhaps they were too distracted by the mire of their circumstances to see God's bigger plan for them. Is that what's preventing you from embracing the abundant life God's laid before you?

As the years have revealed greater hope in Franklin's changed life, something more important has happened—*he's* been transformed. His behavior isn't always perfect, and his reactions aren't always rational, but there's no doubt he's a different, happier dog than the pup that first arrived in our home. He no longer cowers at unexpected movements or jumps at sounds we make because he's discovered the assurance of his new life. His new life has made him new.

The greatest victory of God is not in changed circumstances but in changed lives.

Key Themes

New life, Transformation, Trials

CHEW ON THIS: QUESTIONS FOR YOU AND YOUR PACK TO GNAW ON

Reflect on the phrases or concepts that stood out to you in this chapter.

1. Read 2 Corinthians 5:16-19. In what way is Christ transforming you into a new creation?

2. Read James 1:2-4. Reflect on a trial from your past. How did God use that trial to draw you closer to Him or transform you?

3. How should those reflections affect the way you view the people and circumstances in your life now?

6

WEAR YOUR JINGLES

Do you know who you are? I've asked God why I have to be me rather than someone else through the blurred perspective of tear-filled eyes. My disappointment, He revealed, was in a person who didn't exist. I was not the person I'd brought accusations against. My self-doubt rooted itself in a misunderstanding of who I am. My experiences led me to believe the things I accomplished determined my identity, and according to my measuring stick, I had accomplished little.

The first thing we gave Franklin was not a ball or plush toy. It wasn't a blanket to comfort him or a dish to feed him. We had those things prepared, but our first gift to Franklin was a thin red collar with a name tag attached to it. I inscribed his name on one side of the bone-shaped plate with my name, address, and phone number on the other.

After adjusting the length of the collar, I reached down and placed it around his neck. Franklin gave a quick, startled jump when the buckle clicked into place. What was this thing? I moved my hands away, and he shook his body as if he were trying to dry off after being splashed. He was curious for a few minutes, but it didn't take long for him to become accustomed to the collar and move on. He likely would have preferred the ball.

This gift, however, was a more lasting offer—the gift of identity. The tag not only identified who Franklin was but to whom he belonged. It was a proclamation of ownership and belonging that would prevent him from ever getting lost. For those who belong to Christ, God's also inscribed our names and placed His identity upon us:

> Now it is God who makes both us and you stand firm in Christ. He anointed us, set his seal of ownership on us, and put his Spirit in our hearts as a deposit, guaranteeing what is to come.
>
> 2 Corinthians 1:21-22 NIV

Over time, Franklin's apathy toward our gift changed. He's come to love the bond we share putting his collar on each morning. He may not know what they say or understand their purpose, but he knows the tags are special. We call them his jingles. When we shake them and call out, "Time to put on your jingles," they ring out a beckoning call to him. He runs to us from wherever he is in the house so he can wear them. The sound of his paws gallop through the halls with each determined step he takes. When he appears, Franklin elongates his neck by pushing his snout into the air so his daily collar ceremony can knight him once again. He's drawn to them just as we should be drawn to our identity in Christ.

The jingles are a symbol of who Franklin has become in his adoption. His vaccination tag shows that he's protected, and his name tag proclaims who he is and to whom he belongs in this world. But his collar doesn't have two name tags, one with his name and another to identify his owner. He has one tag that bears both our names. It's one identity, inseparable. We too often try to separate who we think we are from the name of Jesus. "But whoever is united with the Lord is one with him in spirit" (1 Corinthians 6:17 NIV). We only disparage ourselves when we try to remove our name from the new identity He's given us.

Perhaps we resist accepting the new inscription on our lives because we don't think we're worthy, or maybe it's because we fear the new responsibility of bearing His name. Once Franklin leaves the house with his jingles on, he not only carries his own name, but our name as well. He becomes a representative of that identity. Franklin has struggled with anxiety and fear-based behavior for most of his life, so there are times when his actions outside the home more closely resemble the old life he came from rather than the new life his tags represent. On some outings, he may disobey our commands, bark at another dog, or try to pull us in a direction of *his* choosing. On other days, he'll walk calmly next to us, repeatedly looking up for our direction. In either case, his actions are more a reflection on us than on him.

When we see a dog or even a child out of control in public, isn't our tendency to look to the owner or parent? The same is true when you identify as a child of God, but even more so because we're created in the image of God (Genesis 1:26-27). Our behavior affects how non-believers view Christ.

In the moments when Franklin loses control, it's because he's forgotten who he should turn to for direction.

His emotions have overwhelmed the memory of who he belongs to in that moment. He's forgotten his new identity.

Imagine how much easier it would be to ignore the labels put on us by others if we constantly lived in the identity Christ has given us. "For we are God's masterpiece. He has created us anew in Christ Jesus, so we can do the good things he planned for us long ago" (Ephesians 2:10 NLT). When people watch the way we live our lives and look at our tags, how will they respond? Do our actions represent our old life or the new? God's desire is to embrace us as His own, counting the righteousness of Christ toward our new nature. Whose jingles are you wearing?

Key Themes

Adoption, Behavior, Identity

CHEW ON THIS: QUESTIONS FOR YOU AND YOUR PACK TO GNAW ON

Reflect on the phrases or concepts that stood out to you in this chapter.

1. Review 2 Corinthians 1:21-22. What does it mean to have God set His seal of ownership on you?

2. How would it change the way you view yourself if you could fully embrace this truth?

3. What evidence has there been that God has entrusted you with His identity in your life?

4. Read 2 Corinthians 5:20. How does knowing we are Christ's ambassadors to the world change your perspective?

REGULAR GROOMING

Franklin had a new identity and a new life. We'd even cleaned up the initial mess hidden in the trunk of our car. But that didn't erase the suffering he'd endured before we rescued him. If you see a picture of Franklin today, you'll notice an adorable forever-puppy face attached to irresistible fluffy ears and a body of thick black curls. If you look closely, he also has a small patch of white hair running up his chest, silky to the touch like the edging on a baby's blanket.

As you can imagine, he wasn't so well put together when he first joined our family. He had an awkward cuteness that showed undeniable promise, but it would take time to nurse this neglected little pup back to full health. Still, he had an adorable quality to him with puppy hair so light it moved in the air without a breeze, delicate and soft. There was little doubt Franklin would become a handsome pup, but his outward appearance was only a cover for his past.

The shelter told us about Franklin's history, but the evidence of his difficult life became more apparent the first time we gave him a bath. We placed towels on the floor and ran the water in the tub to be sure it was the right temperature. We placed the oatmeal puppy shampoo and organic conditioner for dogs on the side of the tub and closed the bathroom door should he try to escape.

We placed him in the tub, and to our surprise, he didn't mind being bathed at all. He edged closer to us and sniffed the air, reveling in the attention. A wonderful family moment was developing until the realization of what we were seeing sobered the experience. As we used the detachable shower head to run the water over him, his airy curls fell straight along his body, revealing his hidden skin. The warm water ran over my hand as I gently moved my fingers along his side. Gina and I shared a glance of sudden sorrow. Now we could see just how much Franklin had suffered. All this cuteness was covering a body full of scars—the remnants of abuse, neglect, and disease. The past had left its mark.

Does our outward appearance shield the world from our past and current struggles? I don't mean our physical appearance, but the part of us we allow others to see. Just like Franklin, our new identity can temporarily hide our brokenness from people rather than using our community to find healing. Even more concerning, sometimes we not only hide our trials from other Christians, but we try to conceal them from God and even ourselves. That's why the fourth principle of Celebrate Recovery's plan for discipleship and healing challenges each believer to "Openly examine and confess my faults to myself, to God, and to someone I trust." There's a difference between ignoring our scars and moving forward from their quiet hold over us.

That's how silent suffering works in the life of a Christian. We cover up our scars, pretending they're not there, showing the world something more attractive as we try to convince ourselves the scars don't exist. The scars might be from past trauma or someone inflicting harm on us, but they could also come from our own actions, a secret life of sin we've carried.

Too many people in our churches believe they need to wear an emotional mask to be a good Christian, but nothing could be further from the truth. Jesus did not willingly surrender His life because we were adorable, but because He saw the scars we've been hiding.

> Yet it was our weaknesses he carried; it was our sorrows that weighed him down. And we thought his troubles were a punishment from God, a punishment for his own sins! But he was pierced for our rebellion, crushed for our sins. He was beaten so we could be whole.
>
> Isaiah 53:4-5 NLT

Christ came to heal our scars and restore our relationship with God. He wants to make us whole, but He can't do that if we're pretending our pasts or secret sins don't exist.

Imagine what would happen if Gina and I didn't want to acknowledge Franklin's scars. What if we let him hide his past by never giving him another bath? What if we only focused on how cute Franklin appeared and ignored new injuries as they occurred? That would be detrimental to his health, and we love him too much for that.

There's a continual cleansing and grooming that occurs for us after Jesus has rescued us. Theologians call it sanctification. It occurs as we learn to trust in God's character by pursuing an honest relationship with Him and members of our church family. God will make you beautiful beyond your outward appearance. He won't cover your scars; He'll replace them.

People will see a radiance in your life when God is the one cleaning your deepest hurts. And the story of your healed scars, the ones God used to draw out a greater beauty in you, will draw others into Christ's rescue for them.

If you're a rescue pup, you can't get clean without revealing your scars.

Key Themes

Cleansing, Confession, Your Past, Sanctification

CHEW ON THIS: QUESTIONS FOR YOU AND YOUR PACK TO GNAW ON

Reflect on the phrases or concepts that stood out to you in this chapter.

1. What scars from your past or current injuries have you been hiding?

2. Read Hebrews 10:22-25. How can you apply this passage to your own life?

3. What qualities would you look for in a person to help you seek God's healing? Ask God to reveal that person to you.

8

A LEASH ON LIFE

Having an unleashed soul doesn't mean we live without restrictions. The question is whether we're wearing the world's choke collar or the guiding harness of God's plan for our lives. We only find true peace in the confines of healthy boundaries. I may set some boundaries in my life, but many of them are put in place by others. Imagine what might happen if I, as a pastor, approached the trustees of our church and said, "I have freedom in Christ, so I'll only be working once a quarter. I'll let you know which days I pick." That might prompt a longer discussion with the executive pastor and Human Resources, don't you think? Freedom in Christ gives us victory over the shackles of condemnation and slavery to a law impossible to follow. It doesn't free us from responsibility or God's guidance.

Franklin did not immediately take to walking on a leash. On a good day, his struggle took the form of dragging us behind him, forcefully trying to dictate our path. He'd pull so hard he'd cut off his own air supply, choking, gagging, and wheezing as he continued to blaze forward. He was causing himself harm by trying to take control.

His anxiety made it impossible for him to grasp the purpose of the restraint. Franklin only saw the confinement of the leash and ignored the greater purpose of its protection. I wonder how many times I've caused myself harm by fighting against the restrictions of safety God has placed on my life?

Unfortunately, pulling was not the only problem Franklin had while walking on leash. He got along with some dogs but displayed fear-based aggression toward many others. This not only caused behavioral challenges but also a potential danger since Franklin appeared to have size-blindness. To him, a Rottweiler or Doberman seemed a perfectly reasonable opponent for a miniature poodle throwing a tantrum. Upon seeing another dog, he would go into a frenzy, take the leash in his mouth and thrash it back and forth like a shark with a seal in its jaws. With growling and gnashing of teeth, he'd only break long enough to lunge at the unsuspecting dog. My body tensed with the fear he might hurt himself as he threw his body to the ground, fighting to get away from the leash.

Our trainer later explained that Franklin's violent display came from feelings of fear, not of the leash, but a fear of being out of control. He felt responsible for everything going on around him, and until he could trust us to take charge, he would continue to act out. We began a series of exercises that allowed Franklin to keep his focus on us rather than his surroundings. But the exercises didn't take place outside as we peacefully strolled through an open field. Instead, they took place in our home.

The trainer showed us a series of training techniques designed to refocus Franklin's attention on us when he wasn't sure what to do. In the beginning, we simply trained him to look at us for confirmation before getting up from a sitting position.

At first, that seemed confusing to me. How would this help when a random Shih Tzu walked by Franklin in our neighborhood? How would he learn to behave outside if we didn't train him outside? But our trainer taught us, rather patiently, that Franklin needed to learn how to follow our leadership in the safety of our house before he could be expected to follow us with all the distractions of the world.

Our relationship with God is no different. Does the uncertainty of our lives make us look to God or pull away from Him?

When challenged by the actions of others, too many of us attack our leash rather than our fears. As followers of Christ, we can't wait until we're triggered by the difficulties of life to seek God's direction because once that's happened, we're already out of control. That's why we should engage in the daily exercises that teach us how to trust His guidance through our fear. The psalmist wrote:

> I have refused to walk on any evil path, so that I may remain obedient to your word. I haven't turned away from your regulations, for you have taught me well ...
>
> Your word is a lamp to guide my feet and a light for my path.
>
> Psalm 119:101-102, 105 NLT

Teaching Franklin to focus on us rather than the situations he encountered didn't actually change the circumstances. He still crossed paths with other dogs, and he often found himself surrounded by things that could be dangerous. The goal of his training was not to change the world itself but to change his perspective of who was in control.

Sometimes we view the leashes in our lives as a restraint rather than God's protection for us. The Psalm above describes a heart of gratitude in submission—a recognition of the Father's authority. How often do the anxieties and trials of this world cause us to lash out in fear or anger? God wants to offer us a clear path and the confidence to believe He can handle anything we encounter on that path.

It's impossible for chaos to produce an unleashed soul. A life without structure or boundaries will only create anxiety and uncertainty. A life tethered to the world will bring oppression and self-doubt, but embracing the restrictions and guidance offered by God will give us security and peace. That's true freedom. Who or what are you allowing to lead you?

Key Themes

Control, Leadership, Surrender, Trust

CHEW ON THIS: QUESTIONS FOR YOU AND YOUR PACK TO GNAW ON

Reflect on the phrases or concepts that stood out to you in this chapter.

1. Can you identify a leash God has put on your life for your protection? How does thinking about that restriction make you feel?

2. Have there been times when you've pulled against the way God was leading you? If so, how did it affect you?

3. Read Psalm 23 and, if you're familiar with the passage, ask God to show it to you with new eyes. How would your life be different if you allowed God to direct your path?

4. What practices or exercises would help you give up a desire for control and trust God?

THE PACK WALK

With continued training, Franklin started looking to us for direction rather than his own instincts. As he gained confidence, our trainer introduced us to a service she provided called Pack Walks. It was time for Franklin to face his greatest fear—other dogs. Franklin feels threatened by the dogs he encounters during his daily walks, but she explained how dogs were designed to travel in packs. Movement and community are key to the pack mentality, and she believed Franklin could have greater success assimilating to a larger group of dogs moving together.

We were nervous when we brought Franklin to his first session. How would he react? Would he lash out at another dog? Would he *bite* another dog? I felt an uncomfortable flutter in my chest as I parked the car near the old baseball field. Franklin whimpered in the backseat, echoing my own anxiety.

As we walked into the park and saw the other dogs mingling in the distance, it was obvious Franklin felt out of his element. His puffy stub of a tail which usually moved back and forth with vigorous joy, tucked itself downward in retreat. Franklin's nervous gaze was one of uncertainty. We moved with trepidation across the long field. Franklin pulled on his leash and cried as we got closer to the rabble of strange dogs ahead. We arrived just as the trainer was placing the dogs in a carefully crafted line, each dog in a specific spot based on their size and temperament. This offered structure, but Franklin was restless.

"Oh, good. Franklin's here," the trainer said, pointing to a place in the middle of the line for us to join. I gripped the leash tighter, which only transferred my fear to Franklin.

This is a terrible idea, I thought. *We've made a horrible mistake bringing him here*, but before I could verbalize my feelings to Gina, the pack started moving. As the more experienced dogs led the way, Franklin's demeanor calmed, and an immediate change came over him. He lifted his head and trotted along with the members of his new group. My eyes widened as I looked at Gina, and she reciprocated with a silent acknowledgment of her own surprise.

Yes, Franklin was leery of dogs that got a little too close at first, but dogs that would have thrown him into a frenzy if he'd met any of them on the street were surrounding him on all sides. Yet he walked along. And rather than fighting, he took on the disposition of the larger pack. As soon as he took part in a community of other dogs moving together in the same direction, his temperament changed.

It didn't take long before Franklin wanted to be at the front of the pack, but it was important for him to follow before he could lead. That's a lesson for another day, but the group they had placed him in was changing his perspective.

Like Franklin, God created us to live in community. And just as we saw modeled in the pack walk, we take on the characteristics of those we surround ourselves with each day.

> Don't befriend angry people or associate with hot-tempered people, or you will learn to be like them and endanger your soul.
>
> Proverbs 22:24-25 NLT

As we grow in a relationship with Christ, it's important we find other Christians to move forward with. Besides taking on the characteristics of those we associate with, there are three important lessons we can learn from the pack walk.

The first is the concept of movement. Franklin retreated to his natural state of anxiety before the group started moving. A true Christian community is always moving toward God with their eyes on Him asking, "Lord, where are we going next?" The community we choose should take continual steps toward God, both individually and as a group. Moving together makes it much easier to stay on course.

The second is that a pack mentality doesn't erase the uniqueness of your own personality. It will focus the purpose and mission of the pack while providing safety, but it's still made up of individuals. Those with leadership skills will naturally move to the front of the pack, those filled with encouragement will move through the group greeting others, and shepherds will move to the edge of the group to make sure everyone stays together, moving in the right direction. Franklin became friends with a small Chihuahua named Señor, whose personality differed greatly from his own—bold and confident. This was not a Chihuahua meant for a Beverly Hills purse. Even though they were very different, they enjoyed the journey of their pack walk together. They moved in unison as distinct individuals. Each dog in the pack maintained his personality while conforming to a purpose greater than himself.

Finally, there's a difference between a pack mentality and a mob. Mobs seek destruction rather than harmony. Unfortunately, you can find both in the Church. So it's important to remember a mob may well disguise itself as a pack when you're evaluating healthy communities to join. A mob may even call themselves a pack, but there's a very important difference; a mob is made up of individuals with selfish ambitions, using the cloak of numbers to cover their own behavior. This can bring a false sense of belonging but results in emptiness and pressured conformity to harmful behaviors. A pack is interested in the good of the entire group, making each individual better.

What influence do the people in your life have on your decision making? Purpose is revealed in community. Relationships either encourage us in our communion with God or they draw us away from Him. They help refine us for the mission God's given us, or they distract us with selfish desires and ambition.

Ultimately, you will have to join a pack of some kind. Be sure you know what pack you're running with.

Key Themes
Community, Discipleship, Following, Relationships

CHEW ON THIS: QUESTIONS FOR YOU AND YOUR PACK TO GNAW ON

Reflect on the phrases or concepts that stood out to you in this chapter.

1. Read 1 Corinthians 15:33 and Proverbs 13:20.

2. How have your relationships affected your attitude toward others?

3. How would it affect your relationship with God to be more focused on community?

THE TUG OF DISCIPLESHIP

A pack is important to our role in God's plan, but growing to fulfill His purpose for our lives requires more than moving together as a group. It also requires individual relationships with people who will build us up in that calling, mentors who help us break the oppressive collars of the world and train us in the family of God.

While Franklin continued to struggle with other dogs, the structured pack walks were transforming his temperament. Fortunately, Franklin had one safe place where he could spend time with another dog—his regular playdates with Uncle Cole. It only seemed logical that Cole would be Franklin's uncle since he was Gina's fur-brother, the faithful canine companion of her parents. And naturally, Gina's folks would be known by their grand-pup as Grammy and Pépère. That was assuming everything went well when we introduced the two dogs.

We were nervous when we first brought Franklin to visit Gina's parents. We'd just adopted him and didn't know how he'd react to Cole, a large, somewhat clumsy mixed-breed with a licking addiction. His pedigree was never clear, but his Husky-like tail danced with joy, his houndish ears flopped with a carefree approach to life, and his slender, black frame concealed powerful muscles never used in anger. Cole was a lover, not a fighter. But Franklin was so anxious. What would happen when they came together? There were more than a few troubled prayers that their meeting would go well.

We kept Franklin on his leash at first. They met outside in a well-orchestrated introduction. First, we had them meet walking toward each other. As Cole's lumbering body moved toward us on the opposite side of the street, Franklin pulled at his leash with anxious anticipation, but they passed by one another without incident. Then we did several laps around the neighborhood together. Side-by-side they took ownership of the street, each sniffing the patches of grass they found interesting as they explored the neighborhood together. We thought their acclimation would take longer, but this odd couple were drawn to one another, so we moved into the house.

Franklin, unable to reach Cole's towering head, jumped atop an ottoman where he could bring himself face-to-face with Cole. In a gesture that seemed a bit forward to us, Franklin placed his entire puppy-sized head into Cole's mouth, much like you might see a lion tamer do on a vintage circus poster. Franklin then proceeded to lick the inside of Cole's jowls with great vigor. We later learned this is a sign of affection and submission, but at the time, Gina and I just thought it was gross. Gina's mom feared Cole might inadvertently bring an end to Franklin's young life with a single bite down, but the young, rescued poodle and the aging dog became the closest of friends.

Uncle Cole taught Franklin how to play tug-of-war, which is a vital spiritual discipline for dogs. What's remarkable about Cole's discipleship of Franklin was his discernment of Franklin's strength. As they practiced the tug of discipleship, Cole knew the exact amount of pressure he could use to engage Franklin without overwhelming him. He certainly could have whipped Franklin across the room, but he chose fellowship over victory. Franklin also learned the all-important release command, which is actually what makes the game a discipline. Once you find community, it's important that you also find individuals who will invest in helping you grow. "As iron sharpens iron, so a friend sharpens a friend" (Proverbs 27:17 NLT).

As their love for one another became evident, Franklin started visiting Uncle Cole every Wednesday for a playdate. This also meant we spent more time at their house. Gina and I had dinner with her parents when we came to get Franklin every week. Discipleship has a tendency to create a shock wave of healthier relationships. A discouraged fellow pastor once lamented to me via Twitter that, "replication is the hardest part of discipleship." I tend to think that's only true when you make replication its goal. If you focus on the health of the tree, fruit is the natural result.

Franklin has never been a dog we could allow off-leash. His ability to become distracted is unparalleled, and he could easily wander into traffic or find a coyote to challenge. The only regular exception was when we'd roll up to Gina's parents for his weekly visit. We'd pull into the driveway, and I'd open the back door of the car and firmly say, "Wait."

He shook with excitement as he tried to remain seated in the back of the car, anxiously waiting for me to give him the command. Once released, he'd jump out of the car and sprint to the garage door, running back and forth like a sugared-up toddler trying to get into the cookie cabinet. The moment the door started to lift, he'd squeeze his body under the frame to get inside. Franklin was learning how to be part of a family, and he couldn't wait for his next meeting with Uncle Cole to start. I wonder how our lives would be different if we were that excited to find someone who could speak into our lives? Have you been intentional in finding another person to guide you to a deeper understanding of what it means to be in the family of God?

God put Philip in the path of an Ethiopian who was struggling to understand Scripture.

> Then Philip ran up to the chariot and heard the man reading Isaiah the prophet. "Do you understand what you are reading?" Philip asked.
>
> "How can I," he said, "unless someone explains it to me?" So he invited Philip to come up and sit with him.
>
> Acts 8:30-31 NIV

The man recognized he couldn't learn how to understand what God was saying to him without a mentor, and he invited Philip to be his guide in understanding Christ's saving grace. Philip didn't hesitate. He ran to encourage someone in the faith.

That was true of Cole's relationship with Franklin too. As they spent more time together, it was obvious Franklin wasn't the only one gaining something from their friendship. Cole showed glimpses of a long forgotten puppy-hood during their visits. He jumped and teased and played in ways he hadn't for years. He'd re-encountered joy. While Cole often had to spend an entire day sleeping after Franklin upended his peace, there was a new animation in his spirit as he played with Franklin and taught him how to become a family dog. That's God's desire in our relationship with other Christians. There should be a livening of the spirit as we have fellowship, equip, and build one another up.

As an endnote and to be clear, this is not a perfect analogy. It is never appropriate to lick the inside of your mentor's mouth.

Key Themes

Discipleship, Friendship, Spiritual Growth, Mentor

CHEW ON THIS: QUESTIONS FOR YOU AND YOUR PACK TO GNAW ON

Reflect on the phrases or concepts that stood out to you in this chapter.

1. Read John 15:10-11. How does this passage relate to discipleship? What should the result of discipleship be?

2. Are you seeking out individuals who can help you grow spiritually? What are some ways you can build those relationships?

3. How could you be more intentional about investing in someone else and finding others to help you grow?

FETCH
AND OTHER SPIRITUAL GIFTS

I t took Franklin some time to grasp the concept of playing tug-of-war. Even today, he rarely gravitates toward it. As we watched Franklin learn the complexities of this new game, we remembered the discovery we made on his first day with us. Given the difficult nature of his first few months, we were unsure if he knew how to play at all. There were, however, some things he seemed to have a natural talent toward.

Friends told us it's best to introduce a puppy to your house in stages, gradually giving them access to more and more rooms in the house. We started Franklin off in the kitchen since that would be the easiest place to clean up any accidents. So on our first day in the house with him, we put a baby gate up to cordon off the kitchen and made up a little area for him under the window. We sat on the linoleum floor as he explored the room.

His tiny body moved along the edge of the counters with uncertain steps, sniffing along the floor. When he reached the refrigerator, he seemed momentarily confused. Everything was new, and he was equally distracted and intrigued by each new corner or furniture piece he approached. At first, he appeared less interested in us than scent-hunting around the space. When he finally noticed me again, he waddled across the floor to where I was sitting and placed one paw on my folded legs.

I was holding a mini stuffed octopus a friend had made for Franklin's arrival, and after looking up at me, his eyes brightened as he extended his nose toward the plush cephalopod with inquisitive interest. He pawed at the toy in my hand and made small, awkward bites of exploration on one of its eight legs. Not expecting anything, I tossed the purple octopus to the other side of the kitchen. Franklin chased it, sliding on the floor as he reached the place where it landed. Then, as if he'd been doing it for years, he picked up the toy, trotted back, and dropped it in my lap.

His wide black eyes looked up at me as if to say, "Can we try that again?"

Over and over, I tossed the toy. Again and again, Franklin brought it back and dropped it in front of me. And each time the toy left his mouth, his gaze turned to me for approval and an expectation that we would keep playing. Every time his eyes asked for another throw, I felt our bond grow deeper. He had a natural inclination for fetching, and he loved it.

Franklin is not alone. As Christians, we all have gifts designed to help draw us closer to the Father and serve others.

There are different kinds of spiritual gifts,
but the same Spirit is the source of them all.
There are different kinds of service, but we

serve the same Lord. God works in different ways, but it is the same God who does the work in all of us. A spiritual gift is given to each of us so we can help each other.

1 Corinthians 12:4-7 NLT

There are individual talents God builds into us from birth—natural abilities. And those talents often feed into a supernatural gifting He gives us through the Holy Spirit when we become believers. When we use those gifts and talents, it builds our intimacy with God and brings Him joy.

The book of Zephaniah reveals God's character and feelings toward His children when the prophet describes how God reacts to the people of Jerusalem by writing, "He will take delight in you with gladness. With his love, he will calm all your fears. He will rejoice over you with joyful songs" (Zephaniah 3:17 NLT). That's how I felt as I watched Franklin excel at something he was accomplishing under my direction.

Do you view your gifts as a tool to complete tasks, or do you view them as an intimate connection with the Father? Do you run back to Him every time you use them, excited to see what direction He'll send you next?

Franklin plays fetch every day. *Every day.* In fact, he's insistent. It doesn't matter if I'm trying to read or get ready for work; he wants a few moments to play fetch with me every morning, and he doesn't relent until he gets that interaction. Wherever I am, he seeks me out and drops a toy at my feet. When I pick it up, Franklin leaps on his hind legs with joy.

"Sit," I say to him. "Wait." He does his best to settle his body into the sit position, but he quivers with excitement. It's the purest type of happiness.

As I finally fling the toy across our living room, he falls over himself to chase after it. He returns with each toss, offering me the toy, and looking to me for direction.

Seek.

Wait.

Go.

Return.

Seek direction.

What if we all used our talents in that way?

Key Themes

Joy, Serving, Spiritual Gifts, Talents

CHEW ON THIS: QUESTIONS FOR YOU AND YOUR PACK TO GNAW ON

Reflect on the phrases or concepts that stood out to you in this chapter.

1. Read 1 Corinthians 12:4-31 and Romans 12:6-8. What spiritual gifts do you sense the Father has given you? (If you don't know, ask Him to reveal them to you, and consider taking a spiritual gifts assessment test through your church.)

2. How have you used your talents and gifts to serve others and grow closer to the Father?

3. Do you look to the Father expectantly for direction when using your gifts? What would happen if you did this more intentionally?

MAN'S BEST FRIEND

Another one of Franklin's abilities, one that's more in line with human gifts than playing fetch, is compassion. If you've ever experienced the love of a dog, you know they have an incredible sense of empathy for human suffering. Many have the uncanny ability to know when someone is sick or troubled. They sense pain and respond with unconditional love. Perhaps that's why dogs are considered man's best friend—their love intensifies in the fire of our adversity.

As human beings, we sometimes struggle with how to respond to someone else's suffering, but God unleashes our soul for the purpose of showing compassion to others. It's impossible to gain true freedom without gaining a consuming empathy for those who are still in bondage. Whether their chains are spiritual, emotional, or physical, the more attuned we are to the suffering of others, the greater opportunity we have to honor the abundant life Christ has offered us. In turn, compassion leads to greater healing in our own souls.

But does compassion mean we're responsible for fixing every problem we encounter? Of course not. That leads to codependency, which we'll address in another chapter. Under the Holy Spirit's direction, compassion may very well lead you to action, intervening on someone's behalf. But when we take action in our own strength, we can make things worse. Have you ever been grieving a loss and had someone say something they thought was helpful but cut into your soul? Not every hurt requires words.

Franklin has experience with both helpful and unhelpful attempts to comfort. He is obsessed with being a first responder. Unfortunately, his first-aid training is limited to licking someone's wound. Despite having watched every episode of *Grey's Anatomy* with us, he still believes he can heal any minor affliction with a good tongue treatment. If I have a cut or a scrape, he'll lose his mind trying to access the injury so he can administer a carefully applied saliva cleansing. I know that's gross and there are very good medical reasons to discourage this behavior, but he'll burrow under shirts or past blankets with the intensity of a prisoner digging an escape tunnel to reach the cut.

Now, there's no lesson we can take from that behavior— or at least there shouldn't be. But in more serious cases of illness or trials, dogs can teach us something very important about conveying care. Franklin proved that beyond measure when I faced a difficult health crisis of my own.

Several years into Franklin's young life, I developed terrible headaches unlike anything I'd ever felt before. The first came on December 22. For a moment, I felt the hallway disappearing and a searing pain as if I were being ripped from my body. I immediately felt nauseous and couldn't focus my vision. Was I dying? Was this some kind of migraine? I'd never experienced one before. Over the next few weeks, the headaches and nausea became more frequent and more intense. I went to doctor after doctor and to the walk-in clinic, but every physician said bad headaches caused my experiences.

By the new year, I couldn't drive or even walk without getting sick. Finally, my wife drove me to the clinic, determined that we wouldn't leave without answers. Although I didn't have all the normal symptoms, such as a fever, my wife insisted they test for meningitis. The doctor emphatically explained that was not likely, but they'd do the test just to rule it out. I'm not sure how long we waited after the spinal tap because they had me heavily medicated, but I remember when the doctor came back into my room and said, "Well, you have meningitis."

Finally, they could start helping me, but it was a long road back to health. I was out of work for nearly three months. In the beginning, I couldn't be out of bed or exposed to light for more than a few minutes. But week after week, Franklin was there the entire time. There was no licking. Instead, he became fiercely compassionate and loyal. He barely left my side. Sometimes he'd get off the bed and sit in the bedroom doorway, staring out as if he were standing guard, but he was never very far away.

He didn't smother me but stayed close enough for me to know he was there. When the medications wore off, I'd shift in pain, closing my eyes tighter and hoping I could force out even the slightest sign of pink light coming through my eyelids. Then I'd reach over to my side. When I touched Franklin's soft hair, I'd feel him stand and move away from my hand—but only because he'd moved closer to lay his head down on my leg or chest. He didn't have any words of comfort or wisdom. He didn't read Scripture passages or bring me cold compresses for my eyes (although I'm grateful my wife did). Franklin couldn't offer any of that, but he ministered to me by being present.

He was there day after day, until I regained my health and was able to move forward on my own. After that long journey with Franklin, I fully recovered from meningitis. But years later, when I again found myself bed-bound for weeks with COVID-19 during the world-wide pandemic, that small dog, without words, became my comforter once again, refusing to leave my side.

Scripture tells us to "Be happy with those who are happy, and weep with those who weep" (Romans 12:15 NLT). Sometimes we shy away from people who are struggling because we don't know what to say or which Bible verses to quote. We ask, "How do I counsel them?" or "What if I say the wrong thing?"

Well, here's something to let you off the leash: Almost nothing you can say in a crisis makes the crisis any better—the fact that you're there does. The truth that came so naturally to Franklin is that being present is more important than what you say or do. Sometimes it's enough to sit silently with someone and share their pain.

How can you be more present in someone's suffering?

Key Themes

Being Present, Comforting Others, Counsel, Compassion

CHEW ON THIS: QUESTIONS FOR YOU AND YOUR PACK TO GNAW ON

Reflect on the phrases or concepts that stood out to you in this chapter.

1. Reflect on a time when someone being present with you meant more than what they said.

2. Read Philippians 2:1-8. What does the example of Jesus and this passage say to you about being present for others?

3. Are you willing to ask God to show you opportunities to be a comfort to others by being present? If so, how can you prepare yourself for those interactions?

COFFEE CUDDLES

Just as God calls us to be present with one another, His greatest desire is for us to be present with Him. Franklin does his own thing most of the day, but he insists on spending time with us first thing in the morning and at night. I often start my Saturday morning by brewing a cup of coffee. With my custom Bat Pastor mug in hand (I may or may not be a superhero preacher on the side), I walk up the stairs to our bonus room above the garage. Looking up for my approval the entire way, Franklin trots beside me with pent up joy. The coffee sloshes in the bat-cup as I nearly trip over his small body. Then comes a warm pressure against my shins as he pushes past. Franklin runs up two steps ahead of me and spins, eager for me to reach the top of the stairs.

"Sit, Buddy. Stay."

I can see the tension in his leap-ready hind legs, and his bottom hasn't fully reached the ground. His obedience to my sit command is half-hearted at best. I get settled sitting in our large, two-person, eggplant-colored lounge chair. He raises his ears, tilts his head, and looks at me, waiting for my release command.

After I put a blanket over my legs, I call out, "Okay!" and Franklin eagerly jumps onto my lap where he joins me every week. We call these weekend meetings our Coffee Cuddles, and it is a moment I look forward to during long days of ministry.

Franklin's favorite way to rest with me in the lounge is in his Leg Nest. He'll wait for me to put the soles of my feet together under the blanket and lay my legs to each side creating a nest where he can curl up into a ball on the blanket between my legs. That's where he's most content. It's safe and comforting to him. I gently pet the curls on the top of his head while sipping my coffee, and he tucks his nose into the blanket with a sigh of well-found peace. The frantic energy he displayed on the journey melts away once he finds rest with the one he was following. Is that how we feel when seeking time with God?

The morning Coffee Cuddles take place in the same place Franklin loves to end his day. Gina and I sit together in the same lounge most evenings, and Franklin loves crawling up to lie between our legs at the end of the lounge. Sometimes he'll bring an antler or toy to chew on, but his real goal is to spend time with us. He rests most of the day, but he longs to rest with us.

I've found I sometimes carve out time to rest during the week, but I'm not resting in God. Leisure is not the same as rest. God wants us to experience a renewal that only comes from curling up in the safety of His love. When we connect with Him, our burdens should melt away. That's the promise Jesus makes to us in the book of Matthew:

Then Jesus said, "Come to me, all of you who are weary and carry heavy burdens, and I will give you rest. Take my yoke upon you. Let me teach you, because I am humble and gentle at heart, and you will find rest for your souls. For my yoke is easy to bear, and the burden I give you is light."

Matthew 11:28-30 NLT

Franklin still has anxiety issues, but his days are much better when he spends dedicated time with us. He doesn't ask a lot of questions. Aside from reminding us to meet his basic needs (like opening the door when nature calls), he just wants to be near us. His behavior and attitude are more grounded when he's able to do that regularly. He receives emotional sustenance from that connection, and that's what God offers us when we rest in Him.

Jesus said, "Remain in me, and I will remain in you. For a branch cannot produce fruit if it is severed from the vine, and you cannot be fruitful unless you remain in me" (John 15:4 NLT).

Do you feel you're growing? Do you feel like your life is bearing fruit? When we feel like we're not making enough progress for the kingdom in our lives, it's not usually because we need to work harder. It's often because we're not resting enough in Christ. When was the last time you pursued God for a time of rest with Him? When was the last time you crawled into a nest of His comfort?

Sometimes Franklin's desire to be close to us can be distracting. He thinks nothing of stepping on the Bible in our lap or lying across our arms when we're trying to read. He seems to delight in pawing away at my laptop, typing a string of nonsensical letters across my screen as I'm trying to write. He's convinced himself he's a world-famous writer like Snoopy, and that one of his contributions will eventually make it into my books. That's what I like to imagine, but in reality, he's just seeking my attention. If I'm honest, I sometimes get frustrated with his insistent attempts to reach me. Fortunately, God never tires of us coming to Him.

I can't imagine how much it would delight God if I pursued spending time with Him with the same level of intensity Franklin seeks time with me.

Key Themes

Abide, Rest, Quiet Time

CHEW ON THIS: QUESTIONS FOR YOU AND YOUR PACK TO GNAW ON

Reflect on the phrases or concepts that stood out to you in this chapter.

1. Read Luke 10:38-41. What does this story say to you about the busyness of life?

2. How much time do you spend just sitting silently with God, listening for what He wants to share with you?

3. How would your life be different if you dedicated a daily time to be present with God?

14

WAIT!

Before I served in the ministry or was remotely responsible enough to have a dog, I had a predictably failed career in the film industry. Predictable because God had called me to serve Him, but like Jonah, I tried to run away from that calling. If you're not familiar with Jonah's story, read the short book in the Bible that bears his name. My story is similar, but instead of being swallowed by a giant fish, it was New York City that swallowed me.

As a struggling artist, my favorite research tool was watching a television program called *Inside the Actors Studio*, hosted at the prestigious theatrical training center of the same name by James Lipton. This was not your typical celebrity talk show, but a scholarly exercise in understanding the art of film.

You wouldn't think Franklin would enjoy such an intellectual show, but he's a very sophisticated pup. Even now, Franklin and I will occasionally watch my collection of episodes with a sense of nostalgia as we enjoy a session of

Coffee Cuddles. In truth, I don't think Franklin cares what we watch as long as we're together and there are no cats on the screen.

With a stack of index cards in hand, Mr. Lipton would interview well-known actors about their craft before an audience of student actors, writers, and directors. After the guest revealed a behind-the-scenes look at their career, the show would end with the actor sitting on the edge of the stage as Lipton asked them ten questions, admittedly stolen from the iconic French television host, Bernard Pivot. The questions were always the same and always asked in the same order.

"What is your favorite word?" James would begin. And after a clever quip from the actor being interviewed, Lipton would naturally follow-up with the second question, "What is your *least* favorite word?"

As I watch the episodes in relative comfort now, I remember obsessing over the same episodes in my roach and mouse infested hovel back then, daydreaming about the answers I'd give Mr. Lipton when I inevitably made my way to his show. That never happened. But if my dusty Screen Actors Guild card somehow landed me on his interview stage, or the success of this book leads Franklin to become the next Rin Tin Tin or Air Bud, I'm afraid we'd both have the same answer to Mr. Lipton's second question.

"What is my least favorite word? Wait."

When I get impatient, my mom likes to encourage me by sharing Scriptures that counter my bad attitude over the phone. You don't realize how many passages in the Bible are about waiting until someone starts challenging you with them. We have an ongoing joke that every verse in the Bible is about waiting.

"Yes Mom, I get it. It's about waiting. They're all about waiting. Genesis 1:1, wait. Genesis 1:2, wait ..."

Franklin and I loathe waiting, but he's become better at accepting the word than I have. That's primarily because he's learned the benefit of waiting. As I prepare Franklin's breakfast in the morning, I ask him to lie down outside the kitchen and wait until I release him to eat. He watches intently, sometimes shifting in place as his eyes remain locked on my actions. When I finally release him with a whisper, he runs to receive his reward.

Our trainer explained that this practice was vital. Franklin needed to learn where his food comes from and who provides for him. The pattern repeats itself when I have a treat for him. I can hold a biscuit in front of Franklin indefinitely, but until I tell him he can have it, his gaze stays fixed on me, and he's willing to do anything I ask of him. Franklin is never more focused on me than when he's waiting. That's often true in our relationship with God, but the reward for waiting on Him is much greater than a cookie.

> Yet those who wait for the LORD Will gain
> new strength; They will mount up with wings
> like eagles, They will run and not get tired,
> They will walk and not become weary.
>
> Isaiah 40:31 NASB

Waiting teaches us patience, reliance on God, and obedience. It reminds us to trust and hope in the promises of God, and it does so by training us to keep our focus on Him. Although Franklin sometimes finds an impatient streak, filling his time of waiting with unproductive whining (which my wife has also known me to do), he's learned that waiting brings him favor with us. He's come to understand the value of waiting and how it brings greater rewards.

When we dream about having an unleashed soul, we often envision a life without restrictions, full of immediate gratification. But that leads to corruption not contentment. God builds our character and our reliance on Him by teaching us how to wait. We need to learn where our provisions come from, and waiting can transform an attitude of entitlement into a heart of gratitude.

The final question James Lipton asks in the Pivot Questionnaire is, "If Heaven exists, what would you like to hear God say when you arrive at the Pearly Gates?"

Of course, we know Heaven exists, and the obvious answer to this question for any Christian would probably be, "Well done, good and faithful servant ..." (Matthew 25:23 KJV). But Scripture continually pleads with us to examine *how* we're waiting as we expectantly anticipate the return of Christ. Whether we're waiting for God's response to something here on Earth or the Son's arrival at the end of the age, are we being productive for the kingdom as we wait?

I'd love to have God fulfill the passage from Matthew with my name when I stand before Him, but wouldn't it be amazing to have God embrace you before giving you your reward and whisper, "Well done, my child. You waited well."

Key Themes

Obedience, Patience, Reward, Waiting

CHEW ON THIS: QUESTIONS FOR YOU AND YOUR PACK TO GNAW ON

Reflect on the phrases or concepts that stood out to you in this chapter.

1. Read Titus 2:11-14. How should waiting for the return of Jesus affect your life?

2. Read Lamentations 3:19-26. How can keeping your focus on God change your perspective on waiting?

3. Read Psalm 123:2. How does looking to God during times of waiting affect our attitude?

4. How can you be more productive for the kingdom as you wait?

15

THE PUZZLE PEACE

D o you ever find yourself chained to things that rob you of peace rather than encourage it in your life? As we learn to wait on God, we'll often find He's trying to accomplish something in our character.

While Franklin's personality flaws require him to work at having successful social interactions with dogs other than his Uncle Cole, he loves children. He's been drawn to them his whole life. When he sees a child on his walks, he always moves toward them, whimpering with anticipation as he gets closer. Once he arrives, I ask him to sit. Franklin calmly complies and lets the child pet him. There are days when he finds himself swarmed by a half-dozen little hands reaching out to him at the same time, but he remains calm, soaking in the attention like sun rays.

"He's so soft," a small voice says in a melodic tone from within the tiny crowd.

Franklin then stretches his head up as if he's helping the child reach him better. Finally, we have to tell Franklin it's time to move on, and with a small lick on the child's hand to say goodbye, he continues on our walk with the strut of a newly remembered confidence.

Even when Gina and I go out alone, it's not uncommon to hear a child shout, "Look, it's Franklin's parents!" We don't have our own names.

We're always comfortable having Franklin around children, but we were a little concerned the first time a friend brought their newborn to our house. How would Franklin react? He'd never seen a baby. If he realized she was a child he'd probably be okay, but what if he thought she was some kind of strange hairless Chihuahua?

Our fears were soon laid to rest. Not only did Franklin know she was human, but he instantly fell in love with her. He positioned himself as close to the baby seat as he could, resting his head on the blanket coming off the side of her carrier. At one point, he even decided he'd welcome her into the household by licking her toes. We discouraged that, but it was clear he was smitten.

The next time he saw his young friend was not until Liliveve Grace had become a toddler. Their reintroduction was one of old friends, and they showed great interest in one another until the Great Puzzle Incident occurred. With enormous excitement, Franklin showed Liliveve his puzzle, a red, paw-shaped plastic form with yellow puzzle pieces that fit neatly into holes covering treats. Franklin loved this puzzle and pawed at the pegs with enthusiasm until he knocked them out of the toy, revealing his reward. As soon as we put the treat-loaded puzzle down in front of them, Franklin frantically swatted at the pieces, knocking them out of the puzzle.

His young friend was not impressed. Didn't Franklin understand you're supposed to put puzzle pieces into place not knock them out? To correct his error, Liliveve started picking up the pieces Franklin had removed and putting them back into the holes. She was undoing all Franklin's work. Undeterred, he knocked them out again. They battled in a silent argument of dexterity—toddler versus pup. With each round, they became more agitated, frustrated by the actions of the other and their inability to achieve their own goals. *Why does this have to be so difficult?* With building defeat, they both struggled with the futility of their efforts.

The Apostle Paul wrote about his own internal struggle, saying, "I do not understand what I do. For what I want to do I do not do, but what I hate I do" (Romans 7:15 NIV).

Perhaps it makes me a bad person, but I found their frustration outstandingly humorous . . . until Liliveve, utterly exasperated, swatted Franklin out of the way. That's when we knew it was time to intervene. The thing that was meant to draw them closer together had completely robbed them of their peace. Have you ever surrendered your peace in a situation that should have drawn you closer to God?

It can sometimes feel as if life is pulling out the pieces we're trying to put in place. We can become overwhelmed by what seems to be untethered chaos. But no matter how much frustration we face, there is no struggle greater than God's strength. Understanding the depth of His power leads to peace. Consider the conclusion David comes to when reflecting on the strength of God:

> The voice of the LORD strikes with flashes of lightning. The voice of the LORD shakes the desert; the LORD shakes the Desert of Kadesh. The voice of the LORD twists the oaks and strips the forests bare. And in his temple all

cry, "Glory!" The LORD sits enthroned over the flood; the LORD is enthroned as King forever. The LORD gives strength to his people; the LORD blesses his people with peace.

Psalm 29:7-11 NIV

I wonder how often we fill our lives with frustration as we try to dismantle what God is doing in our lives by pulling out the pieces He's trying to put in place for us. Sometimes we get so focused on getting the reward that we ignore the larger puzzle God is putting together for us. Could it be that we don't understand how the puzzle even works? Yet we allow the trials and puzzle pieces in our lives to take our peace away rather than allowing God to use those frustrations to refine our faith and draw us closer to Him.

Key Themes

Faith, Frustration, Peace

CHEW ON THIS: QUESTIONS FOR YOU AND YOUR PACK TO GNAW ON

Reflect on the phrases or concepts that stood out to you in this chapter.

1. Can you identify a time in your life when you tried to resist a particular puzzle piece from being put in place?

2. Read James 1:2-4. How can the things that frustrate us in life draw us closer to God?

3. What are some steps of faith you can take now that will help bring you peace in difficult circumstances?

THE JOY OF SAND

In our Christian life, not everything should feel like a puzzle. As we grow, we should see some things more clearly. The evidence of a growing relationship with Jesus is seeing the fruit of the Spirit develop in your life: "love, joy, peace, patience, kindness, goodness, faithfulness, gentleness, and self-control" (Galatians 5:22b-23a NLT).

I think Christians too often strive for goodness or self-control in their own strength and forget we're supposed to have joy in our lives. Joy is the natural result of surrendering our worries to God, so we can only encounter it when we learn to trust Him. That's why Jesus said to the Father, "Now I am coming to you. I told them many things while I was with them in this world so they would be filled with my joy" (John 17:13 NLT).

Franklin really enjoys going for walks and particularly enjoyed visiting the areas around Lake Champlain when we still lived in Vermont. Early one summer, we brought him to a small beach located just off the Burlington bike path. It was still too chilly for humans to enjoy the beach, but we thought it might be fun to see how Franklin would react to walking in the sand. The moment we stepped on the beach, Franklin was taken by a trance-like fascination. What was this loose, pliable ground he'd discovered? He started digging in the sand and swatting at it with his paw. His tail was a blur in his excitement, shooting back and forth at dizzying speeds.

Blanchard Beach is next to a park that cuts off a long, dead-end road, and the tiny beach area has a lot of natural boundaries because of its rocky and tree-filled landscape. We looked the area over and decided it was a safe place to give Franklin a little freedom. It was rare for us to let him off-leash in public, but this seemed to be a fairly controlled environment. I knelt beside him and removed the leash, unprepared for his reaction.

We'd seen him off-leash before because Gina's parents had a fenced-in dog run. Franklin would trot around their yard following Cole, playing with toys or chasing birds. He undoubtedly loved his time in the backyard with Uncle Cole. It gave him a freedom he didn't normally experience living in our condo. But the moment we set him free on the sands of this inlet, we lost our Franklin to untethered bliss.

He was off before I could stand up, kicking sand in our faces as he bolted forward. He raced up and down the beach, darting from side to side with sharp, agile turns so the sand flew up into the air and fell over him as he changed direction. He ran faster than we'd ever seen him move. His ears waved behind him like flags, giving him the appearance of a little black rabbit leaping through an alfalfa patch. He rolled in the sand, sometimes on purpose and sometimes because he miscalculated his ability to stop. Joy. Covered in sand, Franklin looked up at us happier than we'd ever seen him.

God wants us to experience that same unbridled joy, not only in eternity but here on earth. When Jesus described himself as the Good Shepherd, He explained what it means to find our safety in Him:

> I tell you the truth, I am the gate for the sheep. All who came before me were thieves and robbers. But the true sheep did not listen to them. Yes, I am the gate. Those who come in through me will be saved. They will come and go freely and will find good pastures. The thief's purpose is to steal and kill and destroy. My purpose is to give them a rich and satisfying life.

> John10:7b-10 NLT

Jesus serves as a gate of protection for us, and the Father loves to watch us experiencing joy within the safe boundaries of His will and direction. He wants us to discover His character and surrender our cares to Him, because that's what gives us the freedom to live in the kind of joy we saw Franklin experience that day.

God doesn't want us to have glimpses of joy. He wants us to live in continual joy as we draw closer to Him. When Jesus described the importance of abiding in Him, He said, "I have told you this so that my joy may be in you and that your joy may be complete" (John 15:11 NIV). For some of us, it's difficult to imagine living in complete joy. That's because the leashes of this world convince us it's unreachable.

Are there worries preventing you from experiencing the joy God wants you to have in your life? Has your faith become mired by the day-to-day business of a task filled existence? When we can't remember the last time we felt pure joy, it means we're moving away from resting and trusting in God.

Maybe it's time for you to get out on the sand.

Key Themes

Freedom, Fruit of the Spirit, Joy, Safety

CHEW ON THIS: QUESTIONS FOR YOU AND YOUR PACK TO GNAW ON

Reflect on the phrases or concepts that stood out to you in this chapter.

1. What is something in life that gives you abundant joy?

2. Read John 15:7-11. What do you think it means to experience freedom within the boundaries of God's will?

3. What steps can you take to better know God, surrender your worries to Him, and experience joy?

SINK OR SWIM

Franklin has been in love with the beach ever since that first encounter with the sand. We later discovered he's also passionate about kayaking. He stretches his nose toward the sky and smells the air as we paddle around the edge of a large lake. A calmness comes over him as we glide through the water. He loves to stand with his front paws up on the kayak's bow, his light poodle-hair blowing back as he strikes a majestic pose like Washington crossing the Delaware—if Washington had been wearing a life jacket, that is.

Franklin's life jacket is a bright orange vest with two body straps that tighten and lock around his small frame. Double-stitched into the back of the vest is a nylon handle so we can pick him up out of the water should he fall off the kayak.

It may seem over the top to outfit Franklin with such a device, but the precaution is necessary. Franklin may fully embrace the joy of beach sand and tranquil kayaking experiences, but the water itself is another story.

He'll step with caution into a fountain or wade into the water at the edge of a beach, but he has no desire for the water to go above his stomach. He's desperately afraid of being in water over his head. He panics. On one occasion, Gina and I carried him out into water that was a little more than waist deep for us. As I walked away from the beach, I felt Franklin's body become tense in my arms as the water reached his hind quarters. He pressed against me and looked from side to side with uncertainty as the current created by my movement pushed around him. Gina and I stood about ten feet apart, and I gently lowered Franklin into the lake facing her. An expression of complete fear and anxiety overtook him as he frantically paddled toward her. Even though he was perfectly safe, each desperate stroke testified to his perceived fight for survival. Upon reaching Gina, he scrambled up her body like a sailor climbing the mast of a sinking ship.

Franklin's experience was like an encounter Peter had with Jesus when He'd told the disciples to cross the lake without Him. As the disciples were following Jesus' instructions, they encountered a dangerous storm. Everyone on the boat was in peril, but Jesus came to them walking on the water.

Then Peter called to him, "Lord, if it's really you, tell me to come to you, walking on the water."

"Yes, come," Jesus said.

So Peter went over the side of the boat and walked on the water toward Jesus. But when he saw the strong wind and the waves, he was terrified and began to sink. "Save me, Lord!" he shouted.

Jesus immediately reached out and grabbed him. "You have so little faith," Jesus said. "Why did you doubt me?"

Matthew 14:28-31 NLT

Franklin can swim. Poodles were originally bred for water retrieval, and many believe their name came from the German word "pudel," meaning "one who plays in water." That means Franklin was actually designed to be in the water. His fear doesn't come from an inability to swim—it comes from his belief that he can't.

As unearthly as it seems, through His power, God designed Peter to walk on water that day, but it required Peter's complete trust in Christ. It required him to keep his focus on Jesus as he moved toward Him. Fear made that impossible for Peter. Through Christ, his life had a purpose greater than his own abilities, but he had many failures of fear as he discovered that purpose.

One of the cruelest restraints of this world is fear. The effect of fear on our character causes us to make unhealthy choices, limits the influence we have for the kingdom, and makes us doubt God. It robs us of our security and closes doors that were never meant to hinder us. Rather than traveling the journey God has for us, we stop to build our own obstacles in the path. Having an unleashed soul means breaking free from that restraint and moving with confidence toward the purpose God has for your life. The promise God made to Jacob is also available to you.

But now, this is what the LORD says "Do not fear, for I have redeemed you; I have summoned you by name; you are mine..

When you pass through the waters, I will be with you; and when you pass through the rivers, they will not sweep over you. When you walk through the fire, you will not be burned; the flames will not set you ablaze."

Isaiah 43:1-2 NIV

Like Peter and Jacob, many of us fear the dangerous waters of God's call, but when He invites us to follow Him by name, we can let go of the fear holding us in place. As we grow in our relationship with Jesus, we continually discover He's created us to accomplish things we believe ourselves incapable of doing. When we're placed in the water, do we confidently move toward Jesus or do we uncontrollably splash around, trying not to drown? How long will you let fear prevent you from fulfilling the purpose He's designed you for? God accomplishes His greatest works through impossible tasks by ordinary people.

Key Themes

Fear, Miracles, Purpose, Trust

CHEW ON THIS: QUESTIONS FOR YOU AND YOUR PACK TO GNAW ON

Reflect on the phrases or concepts that stood out to you in this chapter.

1. Read Matthew 17:14-20. What do you think prevented the disciples from healing the demon possessed boy? How is this similar to Peter's experience on the water?

2. How does accomplishing a task you've decided to accomplish on your own differ from accomplishing something God has called you to do?

3. Considering the example of the mustard seed, what do you sense God is calling you to do that may seem impossible?

4. What actions can you take to better understand what God is calling you to do as you learn to surrender your fear and trust Him in taking steps toward that purpose?

MOSES SUPPOSES

Sometimes the difference between whether we sink or swim depends on our support system. Just as Franklin believes he can't swim, things in our own past cause us to embrace false beliefs about ourselves. When we look at ourselves or our circumstances through the world's eyes instead of God's, it prevents us from accomplishing the things He's designed us to do. In those moments, it's important to have people who will push you in your relationship with God.

As Franklin showed during my bout with meningitis, there's great value in the ministry of just being present with someone in crisis. But there are other times when we're called to do more, seasons when we must challenge someone to pursue God when the darkness of their circumstances causes them to retreat from His grace.

One of Franklin's closest canine friends is Moses, a gentle giant of a lab with a lethal tail. Named after the playful song, "Moses," performed by Gene Kelly and Donald O'Connor in the classic musical film, *Singin' in the*

Rain, the name is a perfect fit for his character. Like the premise of the musical number, Moses is a little naughty in an adorably endearing way.

Moses and Franklin took to one another very early in their relationship. It was as if they already knew each other. Perhaps their bond formed so organically because "Cousin Moses," as he came to be known, reminded Franklin of his Uncle Cole. Or is it possible Franklin sensed the important role Moses and his household played in his own rescue?

There was a time in my life when I not only refused to walk with God, I actively ran from Him. I never doubted what God had called me to do in life; I just refused to do it. Remember that roach and mouse infested apartment in New York? I thought it was a small price to pay for the fame I was sure to inherit. When I ran away to the city, I reveled in creating a new identity as a "starving artist." How deceived I must have been to believe a lifestyle that minimizes starvation by propping it up as a false badge of honor would be better than what God ad planned for me. When things inevitably turned, I wandered the streets of Manhattan late one night, uncertain if I wanted to see the next day. I even considered wandering into parts of the city where someone might ensure I wouldn't. But a few days later, I took a tear-filled train ride back to Vermont where I stayed in the basement of two very close friends and young Moses.

I was a miserable lump of depression and hopelessness for weeks. I couldn't care for myself and didn't want to. My friends emotionally nursed me back to health and challenged me to seek the God I had talked about so often in the past. And during those weeks, Moses often rested his head on my knee and looked up at me with a compassionate sincerity that's only found in the loyalty of a dog. Labradors, and especially Moses, have a special gift for that comforting gaze of understanding. In time, God used my friends to fulfill this Scripture in my life: "He lifted me out of the pit of despair, out of the mud and the mire. He set my feet on solid ground and steadied me as I walked along" (Psalm 40:2 NLT).

But as that process was taking place, the greatest challenge of each day was getting out of bed. I wanted the world to stop. I wanted to retreat into a cave of quilts and darkness. Moses made that impossible. Every morning I'd hear the door to the basement open at the top of the stairs.

The joyful tone of my friend's voice would then call out, "Moses, go get Josh!" There'd be a brief beat followed by the rapid paradiddle of Moses racing down the stairs with the rhythm of a jazz percussionist.

Then I'd hear the clicking of his claws on concrete as Moses tap danced past the basement's wood stove. Finally, there'd be a second of complete silence—Moses was airborne.

The solitude of my self-imposed isolation was broken by an excited Labrador landing on me with his full weight, forcing his head into my blankets so he could lick my face. His tail wagging with such intensity that it shook the bed, he danced and nudged until enough of his joy rubbed off on me that it forced me from my hiding. That's how every morning started until I could get out of bed on my own.

With his contagious hope, Moses challenged me to move forward when I wanted to stay stuck. And that's exactly what I needed. All this took place before Franklin was born, long before the abuse and neglect he would endure turned him against other dogs. Yet Franklin immediately took to Moses. Perhaps Franklin sensed his encouraging spirit, and that contributed to their playful friendship. Perhaps Franklin understood my deep love for

Moses, knowing Franklin might not have been rescued and I wouldn't be walking with God if it weren't for Moses and his family building me up and pushing me forward.

Either way, the acts of love from one dog allowed the healing necessary for another dog to be rescued years later.

Paul wrote, "Therefore encourage one another and build each other up, just as in fact you are doing" (1 Thessalonians 5:11 NIV). How might the loving nudge we give another believer who finds themselves stuck today affect their impact on the Kingdom years from now? And how might it affect our own healing when God allows us to be part of the story He's writing in someone else's life?

Key Themes

Depression, Discipleship, Isolation, Running

CHEW ON THIS: QUESTIONS FOR YOU AND YOUR PACK TO GNAW ON

Reflect on the phrases or concepts that stood out to you in this chapter.

1. Read Matthew 5:14-16 and 2 Corinthians 5:11-21. How do you think these passages relate to discipleship and challenging one another in spiritual growth?

2. How can you better encourage someone in a dark place to move closer to God?

3. Read Jonah 1:1-3:3. In what areas of your life are you running from God? What has been the result?

4. What practical steps can you take to move forward in what God has called you to do?

OLD DOG, NEW TRICKS

As we stop running from what God's called us to do, He'll begin training us for a greater purpose in His kingdom. And He'll often start this process in the darkest hours of our running. That, however, is not the same as spiritual growth. There's a difference between the things God redeems from our past and the spiritual training required to use those broken pieces of our lives for good. I've met many Christians who believe they're incapable of change, that the task God's placed on their heart is impossible. That may have been true of someone before Christ, but Scripture tells us we become a new creation when we accept Christ's power in our life. "This means that anyone who belongs to Christ has become a new person. The old life is gone; a new life has begun!" (2 Corinthians 5:17 NLT).

When we were training Franklin to go into his crate on command, we didn't see instant success. In fact, the crate was nowhere in sight when we started. We began by placing a towel on the floor. With treats in hand, we stood at the edge of the towel, keeping our focus on the spot we wanted him to be. This confused Franklin. He sniffed the towel and looked up at us, his head cocked to one side and his ears raised. He knew we had treats but didn't understand what we wanted him to do to get them. So he resorted to his old tricks to see if they'd work.

He sat. No treat.

He laid down. No treat.

He tried spinning, but still there was no treat.

He looked up, letting out a puff of exasperated breath as if to say, "I've done everything you've taught me. What do you want?"

Franklin remained perplexed by the towel on the ground and our strange behavior. He didn't understand we were trying to give him access to a new skill. Franklin's not alone. Have you ever felt that way with God, repeating the things He's asked you to do in the past without results? Perhaps He's not ignoring your efforts but trying to teach you something new. We often rely on the skills God's already developed in us rather than recognizing the new thing He's trying to do in our lives.

Each time God brings us to a new level of spiritual discipline, we have a difficult time seeing what's beyond that step. Like Franklin, we can only repeat what we know until God reveals something else in our life. But no matter how old we get, God is never finished teaching us new things. Paul believed that knowing God will never stop working with us should encourage and excite us. He wrote, "And I am certain that God, who began the good work within you, will continue his work until it is finally finished on the day when Christ Jesus returns" (Philippians 1:6 NLT).

Finally, as we kept our focus on the spot we wanted Franklin to be, he let one paw cross the invisible barrier to land on the towel. Treat. Then we waited for him to put both front paws on the towel before giving him a cookie. Next, Franklin had to sit on the towel. And finally, he learned to lie down. As he experienced more successes, we saw his excitement with each new discovery he made. And all this took place before the crate even came into view. Once he had the skills he needed, it was a simple transition to place the towel in the crate and have Franklin willingly walk inside. The final goal became easy because we helped him grow in the skills he needed to be successful.

Franklin loves going in his crate now. We keep it open when we're home, and he spends a good amount of time in there on his own. It's a place of safety for him, but he needed to learn that by trusting us one step at a time.

When God prepares us to do something big, He rarely shows us the final task or how it will happen because He knows we're not ready for that revelation. Instead, He teaches us the individual skills we need to accomplish it. We're incapable of learning everything we need to accomplish God's mission for us in one lesson. We need to learn each step individually, and until we complete the journey, we won't see how the smaller trainings prepared us for the greater mission.

The problem is that we usually desire teleportation over transportation. We want God to bring us to the end of the road miraculously rather than letting Him travel down the road with us. If He did that, though, we'd be completely unprepared for what we'd find at the end of the path. That would be like us shoving Franklin into the crate and pretending he'd learned something. Rather than walking there in obedience and confidence, he'd be frightened and confused. That's exactly how we'd feel if we saw the end of

God's path for us now instead of going on a journey with Him to get there.

Is it possible that God is preparing you for something new right now? Is He waiting for you to take one step onto the towel so He can show you the next step? Maybe, like Franklin, you only know how to spin. You're spinning and spinning, hoping that's what God wants from you, but spinning only makes you busy. It doesn't move you forward. One step toward God can reveal a greater future.

Key Themes

Purpose, Spiritual Growth, Training

CHEW ON THIS: QUESTIONS FOR YOU AND YOUR PACK TO GNAW ON

Reflect on the phrases or concepts that stood out to you in this chapter.

1. Read Philippians 1:6 again. What evidence do you see that God is preparing you for something in the future?

2. How can knowing there's a bigger purpose change your perspective of the challenges you're facing now?

3. Read Hebrews 6:1-3. What steps do you sense God is prompting you to take to further grow your faith?

CHICKEN WINGS AND OTHER TEMPTATIONS

Franklin is not a dog that noses through the trash when no one's looking. He generally has a more discerning and sophisticated palate than that. He never even sniffed around the garbage can, so we didn't immediately recognize or respond to the sound echoing into the living room the night that changed.

There was a hollow thud followed by scraping, like clutter being pushed across a desk. But there was no desk in the kitchen. *What is that noise?* I looked in the sound's direction and squinted my eyes as if it would help me hear better.

With little alarm, I raised my eyebrows at Gina and made my way into the kitchen to investigate. With the trash knocked over and garbage strewn across the linoleum floor, Franklin stood at the opening of the can with something in his mouth. He looked up at me and froze. We were like two gunslingers in the Old West, waiting for the other to make a move.

Apparently, for Franklin, there's one temptation that will induce a dumpster diving mentality—chicken wings. Chicken bones are very dangerous for dogs. They break with sharp edges that can cause internal bleeding or other injuries. Yet the enticing smell of the wings convinced Franklin to engage in dangerous behavior. That's much like how temptation works in our own lives. The sin appears attractive and desirable but causes great injury from the inside once we've partaken. That's why Scripture tells us to run from temptation: "Flee the evil desires of youth and pursue righteousness, faith, love and peace, along with those who call on the Lord out of a pure heart" (2 Timothy 2:22 NIV).

In the kitchen, there was a brief pause as Franklin looked up at me from a motionless stance of proclaimed innocence. The only sound was the hollow rocking of the trash bin cover still coming to a rest from the commotion.

"Drop it," I said, using a command Franklin was very familiar with. Franklin, however, decided he didn't want to flee from temptation in that moment. Oh, no. He ran from me.

In an act of willful disobedience, Franklin bolted out of the kitchen, chicken bone in mouth. I clumsily kicked the garbage across the kitchen as I gave chase, which began a somewhat sloppy pursuit of Franklin throughout the house. I am not known for my dexterity or physical prowess. Gina joined the chase, and we eventually pinned Franklin down, pried his mouth open, and retrieved the chicken bone. To avoid losing his prize, Franklin had tried to swallow the bone. I pulled it out from halfway down his throat. It was not an experience any of us enjoyed.

Once we take a bite of sin, we usually try to hold on to it, too. We blame the devil or even God for putting the temptation in front of us, but the book of James explains where the desire to sin comes from:

> When tempted, no one should say, "God is tempting me." For God cannot be tempted by evil, nor does he tempt anyone; but each person is tempted when they are dragged away by their own evil desire and enticed. Then, after desire has conceived, it gives birth to sin; and sin, when it is full-grown, gives birth to death. Don't be deceived, my dear brothers and sisters.
>
> James 1:13-16 NIV

Having surrendered to the temptation once, the smell of chicken wings still triggers Franklin. We can't put them in the trash because he'll immediately start sniffing around the bin. We need to bag them up and put them in the attached garage where Franklin can't find them. He's even become bolder in his sinful desires, trying to steal wings directly from our plates.

Once we identify something we're susceptible to, it's important that we keep it out of reach. Don't rely on your personal willpower to overcome temptation because you may find yourself running away from God rather than toward Him. As the verse from Second Timothy shows, it's not enough to avoid temptation; we need to pursue righteousness. We're always running toward something, but you can't run toward God and sin at the same time. They live in opposite directions.

Temptation is that small voice that justifies leaving the path you're on with God for an instance of temporary pleasure. "It's only for a moment," the temptation will whisper. But it's easy to get lost once you step off the path.

But if we're willing to listen, God will speak louder than the voice of temptation. "No temptation has overtaken you except what is common to mankind. And God is faithful; he will not let you be tempted beyond what you can bear. But when you are tempted, he will also provide a way out so that you can endure it" (1 Corinthians 10:13 NIV). The question is whether we're focused on the garbage or God's path away from it.

In the spirit of pursuing righteousness, it would be unfair to label Franklin's chicken wing weakness without admitting that the bones were only in the trash because of my own failure to resist them. Along with steak, bacon, brownies, and cookies, chicken wings sit prominently in a list of the top five foods I struggle to defend against in my temptation to use food as a comforting force in my life. It's certainly not sinful to enjoy a chicken wing now and then, but when I go to food for comfort rather than God, it becomes an idol. Franklin's initial temptation was born from my inability to resist yielding to mine. When we refuse to flee from the unhealthy desires that tempt us, it also affects the people around us. It can negatively affect our relationships and cause others to walk away from God on a path we've forged.

True freedom in Christ releases us from the temptations that keep us imprisoned, offering peace in God rather than slavery to our unhealthy desires. We can easily justify our behavior, but what is the tempting scent *you* follow? What desire or behavior overtakes you with such intensity that you're willing to dig through the trash of this world to find pleasure, running from God when He warns you about its danger?

Key Themes

Example, Running, Sin, Temptation

CHEW ON THIS: QUESTIONS FOR YOU AND YOUR PACK TO GNAW ON

Reflect on the phrases or concepts that stood out to you in this chapter.

1. Read James 1:13-18. According to this passage, where do you think the desire to sin comes from? What hope does the passage offer for overcoming temptation?

2. Reflect on the temptations you've failed to flee in the past. How have those incidents affected those around you?

3. What are some ways you might keep the things that tempt you out of reach?

4. Ask God to reveal what temptations you are most susceptible to. What do you sense God wants to do in your life regarding these issues?

21

A GUMDROP NOSE AND BUTTON EYES

Without bias, Franklin is the most adorable pup ever to don a collar. Given the opportunity, dog owners from the Westminster Dog Show or the annual Puppy Bowl might disagree, but they would be wrong. You can send me pictures of your dog if you'd like, but you won't change my mind. When visiting Cousin Moses, it's often noted by his family that Franklin's gumdrop nose and black button eyes make him irresistible. This usually results in him receiving more than his usual allotment of treats. Franklin has also received more favorable treatment with discipline from Gina's parents during his play dates with Uncle Cole. Love may cover a multitude of sins, but cuteness can cover an abundance of mischief.

Aside from the chicken wing incident, Franklin has a taste for the finer things. He longs for the majestic taste of cheese, well-marbled meat, and pizza crust. When these things make their way to our table, Franklin knows whining will not gain him any favor. A well-used expression of feigned innocence, however, can be our undoing. At first, the tiny black paws on the edge of our dark wooden dining table are barely noticeable. Ever so slowly, they are followed by the mussed curls atop Franklin's head coming into view. Finally, he stretches his wide eyes and a hint of that gumdrop nose over the horizon of our table. He looks over the edge as if I've left him in a pit without love, desperately trying to see out from the darkness of his isolation—hoping someone might rediscover his cuteness.

His bad behavior is inevitably rewarded because he's wrapped it in manipulative charm. Franklin has learned how to bypass discipline with personality, but Scripture warns us against the consequences of that approach. "A fortune made by a lying tongue is a fleeting vapor and a deadly snare" (Proverbs 21:6 NIV).

With clever persuasion, there are shortcuts to gain the things we want. We may not have Franklin's perfect face, but most of us learn how to use our positive traits for negative gain. We may not be as intentional about it as Franklin, but we all have tricks we've used to rely on ourselves rather than God.

Do you use humor to cover biting remarks? Have you used material possessions to influence relationships? Perhaps your natural talents have developed into a diva-like mentality where you serve? Maybe you're a smooth talker with a knack for convincing others to agree with you against their best interests. It's even possible you've taken a page from Franklin's book, using your looks to get the things you want. But what does the Bible say about people who act religious but have selfish ambitions?

For people will love only themselves and their money. They will be boastful and proud, scoffing at God, disobedient to their parents, and ungrateful. They will consider nothing sacred. They will be unloving and unforgiving; they will slander others and have no self-control. They will be cruel and hate what is good. They will betray their friends, be reckless, be puffed up with pride, and love pleasure rather than God. They will act religious, but they will reject the power that could make them godly. Stay away from people like that!

2 Timothy 3:2-5 NLT

Using our natural attributes to get what we want may seem natural, a means to an end, but it actually keeps us chained. Luring the mailman into your yard so you can bite him doesn't release you from restraint. It only draws him into your prison and injures him. Culture teaches us to use anything we can to get ahead, but Jesus calls us to live a different life. He said, "You are the salt of the earth. But if the salt should lose its taste, how can it be made salty? It's no longer good for anything but to be thrown out and trampled on by men" (Matthew 5:13 HCSB).

When guests come to our house for dinner, Franklin's misleading performance as the starving orphan in *Oliver Twist* reflects negatively on us. I think his antics are cute when we're home alone, but when Gina and I have a couple over for dinner and those little paws make their way to the edge of our table in front of them, I can often see uncertainty in the eyes of our visitors. Worse yet is when I see a startled look come across their face because Franklin has unexpectedly planted his front paws on their legs, looking up at them to test whether their constitution is as weak as ours. Some fall prey to his adorable trickery. Others see an undisciplined dog.

Just like a rude, unruly toddler in a restaurant, people never look at the child as the source of the problem. The disapproving gaze always falls squarely on the parent of that juvenile . . . or poodle. As Christians, the way we acquire favor in the world also reflects on God. It's a barometer for the health of our relationship with Christ. The favor of God is greater than the favor of the world. But we have to decide whether we want scraps from the world's table or an eternal banquet.

Key Themes

Behavior, Favor, Getting Ahead, Manipulation

CHEW ON THIS: QUESTIONS FOR YOU AND YOUR PACK TO GNAW ON

Reflect on the phrases or concepts that stood out to you in this chapter.

1. Read Galatians 6:7-10. How does this passage relate to the way we interact with the world?

2. What attributes or natural skills might you be using to get away with things you shouldn't?

3. How can you seek favor in this life in a God honoring way?

DON'T SETTLE FOR A ROCK

There's another reason we want to avoid using the charm of our gumdrop nose and button eyes to get what we want—God has a desire to give us a fuller life than we can acquire on our own. It may not be a life of easier circumstances, but it will be a life of purpose, contentment, and joy. When Jesus compared His relationship with us to the trappings of our enemy, He said, "The thief's purpose is to steal and kill and destroy. My purpose is to give them a rich and satisfying life" (John 10:10 NLT). The enemy wants us to use our charm to get the things we think we want, but God wants to provide us with something more.

The difficulty is that we often get distracted from the life God is trying to give us by becoming obsessed with something less desirable. We become so hyper-focused on something we want in the future that we miss what God is offering now.

In our house, Franklin has no shortage of treats or toys. There are times, however, when he becomes transfixed by something out of reach. Sometimes a ball will roll under the couch. It may be there for days, but when Franklin decides he wants it, that's all he can think about. He sticks his tail high into the air as he crouches his head down, frantically trying to dig under the couch. He whines and scratches, only breaking long enough to pace back and forth along the couch like a captive lion trying to reason a way out of his cage.

He'll occasionally look at us with confusion, wondering why we don't help him retrieve the thing he most desires.

"Look, Franklin. Here's a brand-new ball. You can chew the fuzz off this one." I hold the toy out in front of his nose, but the offer only exasperates him. His unhealthy focus makes him blind to the greater things available to him.

"Okay," I say, and place the better thing I have for Franklin on the shelf. We allow him to settle for something less. How often has God had to do that with us?

Sometimes Franklin's obsessions are not only less grand but dangerous. One fall day, while visiting and making s'mores with friends in our backyard, Franklin took an interest in a small, red stone used in the edging of our patio. He began kicking it around the yard by hiking it through his back legs like a college football player. As the flying grass fell back to the ground, he'd chase the rock to its new location and do it again. Over and over, he tossed the rock around the yard.

Finally, he picked the rock up in his mouth and settled into a comfortable position on the lawn. With his paws holding the rock in place, he vigorously chewed on the stone. The landscaping rock was too big for him to swallow, but his teeth were violently scraping it with the sound of chalk breaking against a blackboard. I wrestled it away from him, and when he wasn't looking, added it to the large collection of similar rocks along the back patio.

"Another s'more?" I said to my friends, returning to the circle of human interaction around the fire. But moments later I heard a thud. Franklin had dropped the rock at my feet—the same rock. It had a unique shape, but how did he find it among all the other rocks? Isn't it amazing how keen our senses can become when we're looking for something we shouldn't have?

The sun was setting, so we distracted Franklin and hid the rock among its brothers again. This time deeper and in a darker part of the yard. Once again, his fixation removed any interest in playing with the other toys we'd brought outside for him. He had to find the rock. In less than three minutes, it was lying at our feet again while a small poodle sat looking up at us.

That was enough. This time, I threw the rock over the fence. It was too dangerous for him to chew on or play with, so unlike the ball under the couch, I needed to remove it from his life entirely. His response was not positive, but he eventually accepted the better gifts we had for him. Franklin's life in our home is directed by our love for him. That not only means giving him better things, but removing the things unhealthy for Franklin in order to give him the most fulfilling life possible. To a much greater extent, that's exactly what God has offered us:

> You prepare a table before me in the presence of my enemies; you anoint my head with oil; my cup overflows. Surely goodness and mercy shall follow me all the days of my life, and I shall dwell in the house of the LORD forever.
>
> Psalm 23:5-6 ESV

God doesn't want us to settle for a rock. He doesn't want us gnawing away at something that will harm us or obsessing over things hidden in the shadow of something better He has planned for us. Dwelling in His house brings a greater life of abundance, provision, and peace. There is a difference between what our flesh desires and what God wants to share with us. Becoming free in Christ means releasing the earthly things we're tied to in favor of the greater spiritual gifts God is offering. What are you obsessing over in your own life despite God's promises and provision?

Key Themes

Blessings, Desire, Obsession

CHEW ON THIS: QUESTIONS FOR YOU AND YOUR PACK TO GNAW ON

Reflect on the phrases or concepts that stood out to you in this chapter.

1. Reflect on a time when you became overly focused on something that wasn't good for you. How did it impact your life?

2. How do you think it affects God when we reject His greater gifts for something less that we're fixated on?

3. Review Psalm 23. What type of blessings do you think God wants to bring into your life?

23

THE HOWL OF ANXIETY

Even after we learn to stop settling for rocks, other emotional distractions can prevent us from trusting God's plan for our daily lives. And the Great Dane of those distractions is anxiety.

As we've already established, Franklin has an ongoing and unhealthy relationship with anxiety. We've explored how anxious he is in the presence of other dogs, but there are smaller intrusions on his desire for control that trigger less than positive responses in his behavior. Like other dogs, Franklin does not care for the doorbell. He jumps from his slumber toward the door, desperately trying to force his way through the wooden panels. *Who's here? What do they want? I will destroy them.* The unknown is frightening to Franklin, so he will not calm himself until he knows who's at the door. Then he usually gives them a quick sniff to confirm their identity and goes back to his perch on the couch.

I think that's common among dogs. But Franklin takes his hatred of the unknown to another level. If he walks into a room where we've moved something, it startles him. He tucks his tail, emits a guttural growl, and slowly circles the item from a distance, trying to discover whether it's a threat. Until he knows for sure, he believes it's much safer to assume it is. How often do we respond to the unknown in the same manner? Yet God offers us something greater. "Let the peace that comes from Christ rule in your hearts. For as members of one body you are called to live in peace. And always be thankful" (Colossians 3:15 NLT).

God offers us peace in every circumstance, but we often let fear and anxiety overtake us.

Baby Dragon is one of Franklin's favorite toys. First, he gnaws away at the plush, purple scales running down the dragon's back and tail. Once those have become little more than a remnant of damp nubs and thread, he moves on to chew its wings. He wraps his paws around the dragon's body, holding it down as his teeth tug away at a carefully selected place of weakness in the stitching.

It's all very adorable until he jumps off the couch with Baby Dragon in his mouth and the faint whimper escapes the cotton-stuffed muzzle in his mouth. To the average guest this wouldn't mean anything, but we've seen this before. Franklin is about to spiral into a dark tornado of anxious behavior.

Everyone knows you can't eat a dragon in one sitting, so there's an inevitable moment in Franklin's project when he decides to hide his little friend until his work can continue the next day.

Dragon in mouth, Franklin begins a hurried survey of the house. He paces from room to room, looking in every corner and under every chair for a place to hide the toy. As his eyes dart, his whining intensifies. The volume and desperation escalates as his steps quicken. *What if someone else takes it?* I imagine him thinking. *What if I can't find it?*

Finally, he chooses a spot near the bookshelf, digging at the hardwood floor as if he could bury the toy under the collection of antique Shakespeare volumes. Then, with an exhale of relief, he lowers his head and gently releases Baby Dragon from his previously clenched jaws. With a few final nudges from his gumdrop nose to position his toy perfectly, it appears he has averted the crisis—but only for a moment.

After a few seconds of false contentment, Franklin looks up from the painfully obvious hiding place and realizes this will not do. He snatches the dragon up in his mouth again and moves with even greater intention as the whining grows beyond a comfortable level for the human ear.

Panic. His thinking becomes clouded as his anxiety moves beyond his emotions, completely overtaking his body. He begins to spin helplessly in one spot until the stress reaches such a level of desperation that the Baby Dragon drops to the ground. Franklin throws his head back in frustration and howls—a painful, wolf-like, ear-piercing howl into the heavens. He stops only to take a breath and escalate his cry.

You can call his name, clap your hands, or clang two pots together. There is no sound capable of penetrating his focus on despair. There are only two options: you can let the anxiety run its course (knowing it will return) or you can go over and touch him. That touch breaks him out of his fear, and he looks up inquisitively, confused about what just happened.

Have you ever become so overwhelmed with strife that only a touch from God could break its hold on you? Stress and anxiety is an obsession with control, and our bodies feel the strain when we find ourselves unable to surrender the outcome of our circumstances. But God's desire is to give us peace. That's why Jesus said, "I am leaving you with a gift—peace of mind and heart. And the peace I give is a gift the world cannot give. So don't be troubled or afraid" (John 14:27 NLT).

How would it affect your peace in this world if you started reaching out for God's touch in difficult circumstances rather than a solution?

Key Themes

Anxiety, Fear, Peace, Stress

CHEW ON THIS: QUESTIONS FOR YOU AND YOUR PACK TO GNAW ON

Reflect on the phrases or concepts that stood out to you in this chapter.

1. Read 1 Peter 5:6-8. What part of this passage sticks out to you and why?

2. How could you identify with Franklin in this story? Describe a time when you allowed anxiety or fear to overtake you.

3. What anxieties or fears do you sense God is asking you to surrender to Him now?

4. What do you think would happen if you surrendered those feelings?

CRATES AND CODEPENDENCY

Another source of anxiety can be codependency—a desperate need to gain approval and acceptance from others. That part's not uncommon or even unhealthy for dogs, but in a human being, codependency often manifests itself as a desire to control everything in the person's life, including the lives of other people. Like a Giant Mastiff sharing your couch, codependency can crowd out your joy and peace. This desperate and sometimes unperceived need for validation results in people-pleasing, enabling the dangerous behaviors of others, or manipulating friends and family to gain authority over them.

The anxious paradox of codependency is the pursuit to be accepted and the compulsion to control everything around you. Those two goals seem to be at odds with one another, but they're actually one in the same. For those living in dysfunctional, codependent relationships, controlling the wellbeing of others (or your perception of their wellbeing) feels like the only path to avoid rejection. So, in that craving to be loved and needed, you're constantly on guard, patrolling every aspect of your surroundings, looking for anything outside the realm of your control so no one has a reason to stop loving you.

In an earlier chapter, we discussed how Gina and I helped Franklin become crate-trained. We used that process to explore the steps God often leads us through to teach us a new discipline He wants us to use for His kingdom. But the *how* in our learning is never as important as the *why*. The same is true with Franklin. We didn't train him to spend time in his crate so he'd have another skill, but to protect him from those guard-like tendencies we sometimes see in codependent lifestyles.

When we hired Franklin's trainer to help address his behavior toward other dogs in the neighborhood, she said, "Before we do anything outside, I think we should look at what's happening in the home." For the record, that's never something you want to hear as a dog owner.

For years, Franklin had free rein (and reign) to wander through our house. He barked at every shadow and was constantly on the move. A great deal of Franklin's anxiety in the house, which he carried out into the world, was his need to control and guard his environment. Our trainer (because make no mistake, it was us and not Franklin that needed training) explained that Franklin felt responsible for every room we permitted him to access. In his desire to please us, he felt responsible for the wellbeing of everything around us. This feeling of angst likely multiplied when we left him alone because he believed he was the last line of defense. So he spent all his time patrolling the house, constantly concerned about the areas he couldn't see.

We once came home to find a note taped to our front door that read, "Your little dog was barking all day long and never stopped." Franklin had been in a perpetual state of stress, moving from room to room, window to window trying to protect our home. Every movement or sound from outside was another potential attacker. And all of this was born from a misguided aspiration to please the people he loved. But the task was impossible. How could he protect every room at the same time?

Perhaps we were showing some signs of canine codependency ourselves. We were giving him complete access to the house because we thought it would make him happy. In reality, what we needed to give him were healthy boundaries. That's when we realized crate training was vitally important to his well-being.

Now Franklin hangs out in a 5 × 3 foot playpen when we leave the house. It has a comfy dog bed, a favorite fuzzy blanket, and a pillow that reads, "Home of a spoiled rotten dog." I'm sure you've figured out by now that Franklin is not rotten, but the sentiment of the inscribed cushion is probably accurate. In any case, he loves his crate and has never complained about the pillow's accusation.

We call out the words, "Crate treat!" and we'll hear the hurried tippity-tap of his little toenails moving across the hardwood floor toward his crate. He trots past us into the pen, sits, and looks up at us expectantly. After we give him a little treat, he walks in a contented circle and settles into his blanket. By reducing the area he can access, he's able to spend his time relaxing in his dog bed as he keeps a restful eye over the area we've given him without the fear-inducing need to patrol areas outside his given authority.

Scripture says, "God gave us a spirit not of fear but of power and love and self-control" (2 Timothy 1:7 ESV). That verse is in the context of doing the work our Father has called us to do, but that's impossible when we're obsessed with patrolling areas that are not ours to patrol. Just like

Franklin, many of us try to please God by chasing impossible standards He never asked us to meet. God grants us power in the tasks He's assigned us but requires us to surrender the ones we've assigned ourselves. Stay focused on what God has put before you.

> Let your eyes look straight ahead; fix your gaze directly before you. Give careful thought to the paths for your feet and be steadfast in all your ways. Do not turn to the right or the left; keep your foot from evil.
>
> Proverbs 4:25-27 NIV

We cannot move forward with the unleashed life God has for us if we're constantly distracted by things He's never given us control over. Our desire to control everything leaves us with no control over anything. God has a purpose and a mission for your life. Don't you want to know what that appointment is?

What are you trying to guard that God's clearly placed out of your reach? What's causing you to run from room to room, frantically and unsuccessfully overseeing things God never given you command over? The Father has probably given you a greater area of authority than a playpen, but the healthiest thing we can do for ourselves is to gate off the areas God's asked us to guard and make sure we're on the right side of the gate. As long as we seek approval from people and tasks, policing policies we were never commissioned to enforce, we'll never rest in the boundaries of our divine mission.

Key Themes

Assignments, Boundaries, Codependency, Control

CHEW ON THIS: QUESTIONS FOR YOU AND YOUR PACK TO GNAW ON

Reflect on the phrases or concepts that stood out to you in this chapter.

1. Read Galatians 1:10. Do you think you spend more time trying to please God or others?

2. Who or what are you trying to control? What do you think would happen if you gave up control?

3. What assignments do you sense God is calling you to engage with in a greater way? What spiritual gating-off will be required for you to respond to His call?

25

THE MASTER'S VOICE

As we refocus our energy on the things God's called us to do, we feel more purpose in our lives. That leads to a greater sense of unleashed freedom in Christ. How do we make sure we stay on the right path in that freedom? We must learn to recognize God's voice as we travel.

A dog's greatest desire is to please his master. Man's best friend is happiest when he knows he's fulfilling his master's will. It reduces stress and builds confidence. This is true of most lab and shepherd breeds, and undoubtedly true of Franklin as well—but sometimes he forgets.

One of the great joys in Franklin's life is lying in the sun on our pebbled patio in the backyard. He stretches his body out, reveling in the sun's oppressive heat as if he were a solar-powered pup easing his way into the day. He extends his paws, adjusting his stretch to have the most exposure to the sun's rays. If Charles M. Schulz was right and happiness is a warm puppy, then there's a lot of happiness cooking in our backyard. It is unfathomable to me how lying on the heated rock and concrete of our west-facing patio in ninety-degree heat could be enjoyable to a small black dog. The air is heavy, and the ground feels like a pizza stone baking in a wood fired oven. Yet there he lies.

"Franklin," I call out from the door. "Franklin, come." He pauses for a moment before rolling his head back to look at me, offering just enough movement to acknowledge he heard me without actually following my instructions.

"Franklin! Come!" I repeat with more insistence and a lot less patience, but he just turns his head back to its original sunning position with lethargic disregard.

Jesus said, "My sheep hear my voice, and I know them, and they follow me" (John 10:27 ESV). There are three important elements to that sentence. The sheep know Jesus' voice, Jesus knows them, and they follow His instructions. In the case of the patio paradox, only two of the three are in place. Franklin knows my voice (he clearly knows it when I call him from another room or if I'm just arriving home from the church). I definitely know him. But in this case, he's decided not to follow.

That's not always the case, of course. There are plenty of times when he loves to hear my voice call out his name. Sometimes he'll be curled up on his favorite throw blanket, sound asleep and I'll say, "Franklin, do you want to go upstairs and watch TV?" His ears shift upward at the sound of his name, and by the time I've finished the sentence, he's leapt off the couch and moved with purpose to my side.

Then he looks up at me expectantly with his tail wagging as if to say, "Lead the way."

Later in the evening, my wife will say, "Franklin, are you ready for bed?" Again, from what appears to be a deep sleep, he jumps to the floor and waits for her to start back down the stairs. Certain words will trigger his immediate attention and obedience like *treat*, *walk*, *crate*, *dinner*, and *out*. Some of those may seem like selfish motivations for obedience, but at the heart of those responses is an understanding that he can rely on us to provide his basic needs. His response to other words such as *bed*, *TV*, *upstairs*, and *fetch* reflect his desire to spend time with us. What if we always based our response to God's voice on an understanding of His provision and a desire to spend time with Him?

That, however, brings us back to the sunbathing disobedience of Franklin on the patio. His lounging pose and content eyes are deceptive. He appears happy. He, in fact, believes he is happy, but I know it's not good for him to be out in the sun for too long. It raises his body temperature and dehydrates him. He knows that my voice is the source of his provision, but sometimes he chooses his own path, moments when he hears my voice and decides he will not listen. I will let him stay there for a bit, but I will eventually step out onto the hot slab, pick him up, and bring him inside where he's safe.

God's desire is for us to follow His voice from our own desire to be on the path He has for us. There is a promise to those who listen to His word and obey.

> My son, if you accept my words and store up my commands within you, turning your ear to wisdom and applying your heart to understanding—indeed, if you call out for insight and cry aloud for understanding, and if you look for it as for silver and search for it as for hidden treasure, then you will

understand the fear of the LORD and find the
knowledge of God.

Proverbs 2:1-5 NIV

How often do we hear God's voice but turn toward
the burning heat of something we think we want? The
sheep know the Master's voice, and they follow Him.
The first task in our walk with God is to recognize His
voice and distinguish it from the world's, but then we
must run to His side, look up, and say, "Lead the way."

Key Themes

Hearing God, Obedience, Provision, Safety

CHEW ON THIS: QUESTIONS FOR YOU AND YOUR PACK TO GNAW ON

Reflect on the phrases or concepts that stood out to you in this chapter.

1. Read the story of the Good Shepherd in John 10:1-18. What do you sense God is pointing out to you in this passage?

2. What are some specific steps you can take to better recognize God's voice?

3. Have you ever knowingly ignored God's voice when He was calling you to safety? How did it feel? How could you better resist that temptation in the future?

THE CHRISTMAS THORN

Having an unleashed soul will not prevent us from facing trials. Crisis is a rabid fisher cat, weaseling itself under the fence we've created for ourselves when we feel most secure. It is always unexpected, but it always comes. It's important we learn to obey the Master's voice in the calmness of each day or we'll never be prepared to heed His call when danger comes. Following Christ is essential in the small things of life if we hope to find deliverance from the thorns of sin or spiritual attack.

When comforting the disciples about the crisis to come, Jesus said, "I have told you all this so that you may have peace in me. Here on earth you will have many trials and sorrows. But take heart, because I have overcome the world" (John 16:33 NLT). The disciples had not yet received the Holy Spirit, and they hadn't learned to listen to Christ's voice. So they forgot the instruction that could have comforted and directed them after Christ's arrest and crucifixion. What does that look like in the breath-stealing troubles we face? Do we remember or listen for God's voice?

Much to my wife's dismay, one of my most cherished Christmas traditions is the Great Christmas Tree Hunt. Most people just "go get a tree," but I prefer trudging through the forest for hours, looking for the one tree that calls out to me with Christmas spirit, and then mercilessly sawing it to the ground and dragging it out of the woods. That holiday ritual is the extent of my outdoorsiness, but it's a piece of my childhood I have no desire to see relegated to the yellowing cellophane of an old photo album.

The Hunt is a perfect opportunity for Gina and me to take Franklin on an adventure into the great outdoors, but recently that journey led to a harrowing experience. Finding the idyllic Christmas tree wasn't that complicated when we lived in Vermont, but the elusive and weak-branched trees of the South made the Great Hunt more challenging. After a long drive into the mountains of North Carolina, we spent hours looking for the perfect tree. That mission eventually gave way to searching for an appropriate tree. Finally, even I would have settled for a basic, serviceable tree. No luck.

Gina had gone in a different direction, and since there was no snow on the ground, I took Franklin up a steep embankment. There was no path, and the area seemed unexplored. Perhaps there was a gem hiding in this forbidding landscape. Crammed together, the trees grew out of the thick, twisted remains of dead brushwood and forest debris. Franklin and I fought our way through the dense foliage. I suspected we were the greatest adventurers ever to explore the expansive tree farm. While pondering the manly nature of our winter-jungle trailblazing, I heard a yelp.

I turned. Franklin looked up at me with confusion and fear. A long vine of thorns had entangled his head and legs. He lifted his paw and tried to move, but he was trapped.

Unable to move anything else, his eyes darted back and forth, and a terrified whine broke through his clench jaws.

"Stay, Franklin ... Wait," I commanded. Trying not to pull on the leash that had also become ensnared, my steps toward him were measured and slow.

I knelt beside him and whispered, "Hold still, Buddy."

The sharp tip of a thorn was only centimeters away from his right eye. I exhaled like a sniper calming his body, wrapped my right hand around the back of Franklin's head to hold his chin, and slowly pulled the thorn away from his eye.

The thorns puckered his left ear into a chaotic ball of hair and unyielding barbs. I knew I could free him, but it would take time. I pulled on one of the vine's tentacles while holding the base of his hair, hoping it wouldn't pull, but it did. Franklin panicked. He tried to back away, but the thorns took greater hold.

"Stay still. Don't move, don't move."

He no longer heard my voice. Listening is the first skill we lose when we panic or fight.

He thrashed back and forth, crying with frustration and pain. I tried to steady him, but I only became something else for him to fight. He violently moved his head back and forth and pulled to free his leg. In his desperate actions, he lost his footing and began to tumble down the steep embankment, wrapping more thorny branches around his body as he rolled.

The Book of Proverbs tells us, "Whoever gives heed to instruction prospers, and blessed is the one who trusts in the LORD" (Proverbs 16:20 NIV).

In a moment of crisis, Franklin found himself unable to follow instructions or trust the only one who could deliver him. How often do we resist God's calming voice and helping hand when disaster takes hold of us? Do we wait for Him to remove the bramble of our lives, or do we fight against Him and our circumstances, causing us to fall further into danger and away from His saving hand?

When Franklin's body came to rest, he did not move. He did not cry.

I slid down to where he lay, praying he was all right.

He was breathing normally and slowly looked up at me with surrender. Only then could I free him from the danger he'd encountered. The experience shook him, but Franklin walked away with nothing more than a small cut on his lip.

Many of us seek God after we've tried to walk a perilous path on our own, after we've wrapped ourselves in injury. We look to God only for recovery rather than guidance, but when we learn to heed His instruction with trust at the moment of crisis, we can claim the promise that is so well known but rarely embraced, "Yea, though I walk through the valley of the shadow of death, I will fear no evil; For You are with me; Your rod and Your staff, they comfort me" (Psalm 23:4 NKJV)

Key Themes

Crisis, Fighting God, Listening, Rescue, Trust

CHEW ON THIS: QUESTIONS FOR YOU AND YOUR PACK TO GNAW ON

Reflect on the phrases or concepts that stood out to you in this chapter.

1. Do you remember a time when you fought your circumstances and God? What was the result?

2. Read Deuteronomy 31:6. What does God's promise to Joshua say about God's character?

3. Read Psalm 91. How can you further embrace the promise of God's deliverance and protection?

4. What steps will you take to better trust God and listen for His direction in your next trial?

27

MONDAY NIGHT PAW

When those thorns imprisoned Franklin, he fought against the one person who could help him. We often do the same thing, pulling away from God when we need Him most. But fighting *against* God differs significantly from wrestling *with* God.

Franklin loves to wrestle with his toys. He usually starts by gnawing on them, ripping pieces from his opponent's body like George "The Animal" Steele tearing the stuffing from a turnbuckle pad with his teeth. Franklin whips small pieces of synthetic fur into the air and watches them fall slowly to the carpet. Chewing on your adversary is against WWE rules, but if the referee isn't looking, that's all part of the game.

Gnawing is often how we start our own wrestling matches with God. We chew on the circumstances we're fighting until we realize those trials are actually pressing their teeth into us. "Your enemy the devil prowls around like a roaring lion looking for someone to devour" (1 Peter 5:8b NIV). Unfortunately, we don't always realize how much trouble we're in until we're halfway down his throat. Whether it's spiritual warfare, temptation, or an earthly struggle, we find ourselves separated from God's direction.

Only then do we ring the bell and engage in a wrestling match with God.

In the book of Genesis, Jacob finds himself in that exact position. He'd just escaped from years of manipulation and oppression by his father-in-law, and now it appeared his own brother was coming with an army to kill Jacob and his family. He gnashes the teeth of his fear, doubting God's promise. He mulls his demise, cursing his circumstances until he finally cries out to God.

And then something miraculous happens.

God shows up in human form and wrestles with Jacob all night, not in a metaphorical sense, but in a real physical bout. Now the real battle begins for Jacob. We'll explore the outcome of that match in a few minutes.

When Franklin truly enters the fray, he drops his toy onto the floor from the couch, jumps down and rolls around with what's left of it in his mouth. He stretches his body out on the carpet to get as much leverage as possible, tossing the toy back and forth as he throws himself from side to side. He emphasizes his efforts with a series of short, breathy grunts.

Of course, this is just a game. Franklin wrestles with his stuffed playmates because it's fun, just as my friends and I spent evenings putting each other in wrestling moves like the Roddy Piper Sleeper Hold and driving each others' heads into my mattress with Jake "The Snake" style DDTs when we were ten. Harmless fun.

Like Jacob, Franklin would wrestle all night, but playtime must eventually end. As the self-appointed referee amid

Franklin's free-for-all, I'll sometimes decide it's time to call the match and take the toy away. Franklin often refuses to let go, though, only tightening his grip and turning the wrestling match into the tug-of-war game Cole taught him as a puppy.

There are times, however, when Franklin refuses to let go for a more serious reason—when he's wrestling for my attention. He'll crawl over my legs so I can't move. He'll paw at my blanket until he exposes my arms. Then he'll execute his finisher move, "The Nudge." He'll keep nudging and nudging, forcing himself into my hold until his struggle subsides, and he can rest in my arms.

It was actually God, in the form of a man, who first engaged Jacob in the wrestling match. But once Jacob started grappling with God, he too refused to let go. As dawn approached, God told Jacob to stop wrestling with Him, "But Jacob replied, 'I will not let you go unless you bless me'" (Genesis 32:26b NIV). The prophet Hosea later describes Jacob's encounter with God when he wrote:

> Even in the womb, Jacob struggled with his brother; when he became a man, he even fought with God.
>
> Yes, he wrestled with the angel and won. He wept and pleaded for a blessing from him. There at Bethel he met God face to face, and God spoke to him— the Lord God of Heaven's Armies, the Lord is his name!
>
> Hosea 12:3–5 NLT

Jacob didn't ask for a specific blessing. He wasn't trying to force a particular outcome. He held on to God until the

Lord chose a blessing *for* him, and it probably wasn't the blessing Jacob expected. He'd cried out to God about an earthly circumstance, but God blessed Him with a new name. Israel.

Jacob didn't realize he was in a title match, but because he refused to release his grip on God, the Father transformed his life, and Jacob walked away with a greater prize than he was seeking. Are you fighting against God to get your way, or are you wrestling with God for a new title?

The difference between fighting against God and wrestling with God is whether we're trying to break away from Him or refusing to let go.

Key Themes

Blessings, Fighting God, Wrestling

CHEW ON THIS: QUESTIONS FOR YOU AND YOUR PACK TO GNAW ON

Reflect on the phrases or concepts that stood out to you in this chapter.

1. Read the encounter Jacob had with God in Genesis 32:22-32. What stands out to you?

2. How do you think Jacob is transformed by this encounter?

3. How can Jacob's struggle with God apply to your own relationship with the Lord?

28

GOODNIGHT, SWEET COLE

Cole was eleven years old, and the lump on his chest was not getting any smaller. The vet said it was benign, but his energy was waning.

The only thing that brought a true puppy-like glint back to Cole's eye was his weekly playdate with Franklin. Each time we'd arrive, Franklin pushed past our legs and through the door, ran into the kitchen and checked Cole's food dish. Perhaps his friend had foolishly left a morsel behind. Then Franklin darted into the living room to find his Uncle Cole.

Although Cole ran slower than he used to, and his right front paw sometimes caught on the ground when he tried to lift his leg, they'd run and play together the entire day. Franklin enticed Cole to chase him, and when Cole couldn't keep up, Franklin returned with a playful slide around the corner. It usually took Cole a few days to recover from Franklin's visit, but he blissfully romped about while his young disciple was there.

As the weeks passed, Franklin stopped pushing Cole so hard and seemed hesitant to leave when we came to pick him up. It was as if he knew Cole's time was growing shorter with each visit.

We often talk about grief as if it were a singular event. It's not. The grieving process is a *series* of losses that blur together into an overwhelming, knotted collection of emotions. Oftentimes, except in cases of sudden tragedy, grieving starts long before a loved one dies. Perhaps Alzheimer's or a medically induced coma has stolen the relationship before their last breath can take it. Other times, grief begins with a diagnosis or a loss of mobility that snatches away our hope for a specific plan in our lives. A million small losses in the *now* can stress the coming grief we dread above all else.

With Cole, it was the ever-present tumor on his chest daily reminding us how few days were left with him.

Even when we know the phone call is coming, it's shocking when it comes—not so much a surprise, but a jolting of your spirit. In that moment, the facts we have will not shield our emotions.

When Lazarus died, even Jesus, who knew the state of His friend's soul and even knew He would raise Lazarus from the dead, was overwhelmed with sadness at the news of His friend's death, the suffering of his family, and His anger at the response of others. The Book of John records Jesus asking, "'Where have you put him?' ... They told him, 'Lord, come and see.' Then Jesus wept. The people who were standing nearby said, 'See how much he loved him!'" (John 11:34-36 NLT).

God meant for us to grieve our losses. And though we may not like it, grief is often the fruit of a life filled with love, a testament to the power of our connection with others. But we're taught not to do that. Most of us, at some point, receive the messaging that we should hide our grief in public, that sorrow should have a predictable timeline with orderly stages. It's not true. The pressure to conform to society's needs in our grief is not helpful or Biblical.

Having an unleashed soul means learning to grieve our losses completely and gain the freedom to fall into God's comforting arms with the fullness of our pain. When the world tells us it's time to move on or get over our emotions, it's actually telling us to become a slave to them. But we think they're trying to help, so we push our grief down until it reemerges in unhealthy behaviors and reactions that can affect our health, careers, and relationships.

In the Gospels, we see Jesus cry several times, but it's never a polite sniffle to make the people around Him more comfortable with His grief. Weeping and sobbing punctuated His mourning. Jesus was free to express His deepest emotions and then move forward with purpose.

Franklin's last play date with Cole was on a cold Vermont Valentine's Day. There wasn't much playing, but Franklin gave a card to his Uncle Cole for the holiday, and Franklin received one with a joyful Norwich Terrier on the cover inscribed on Cole's behalf that read:

> *Spending time with you is one of the happiest things in my life! ~Love, Uncle Cole.*

A few days later, we received the news that had been lurking in the pit of our stomachs. Cole was gone. Franklin didn't go to Gina's parents that week. We all needed time to adjust, but he returned for his weekly visit the following Wednesday.

His pace was slower than normal as he entered the house he had visited so often. First, he went into the kitchen where he usually stole some of Cole's food, but Cole's dish was not there. A careful investigation of the rest of the house revealed Cole was not there either. It was a somber visit as Franklin sat with Gina's parents, comforting them in their loss.

Everyone deals with grief differently. Some need to search the house of their lives to be sure the loss is real. Others need to cry or sit quietly. Most of us have a competing collection of emotions that we need to process and untangle. But however we grieve, it's important we allow the process to happen, finding the right spaces and relying on the right people to bear the full emotion of our grief with us.

Scripture says,

> For everything there is a season ... a time to cry and a time to laugh. A time to grieve and a time to dance
>
> Ecclesiastes 3:1a, 4 NLT

Grieving is a natural season of our love for someone. It honors the bond we still have to them. And though our love and sadness endure, our deepest grief is only meant to be a season.

Bottling our grief is the surest way to never escape its grasp. The promise of our freedom in Christ has never been protection from suffering, but to know God's love is greater than our losses.

Key Themes

Death, Friendship, Grief, Sorrow

CHEW ON THIS: QUESTIONS FOR YOU AND YOUR PACK TO GNAW ON

Reflect on the phrases or concepts that stood out to you in this chapter.

1. Though it may be difficult to see while you're grieving, how can the process of grief be considered a gift?

2. When grieving a loss, what is the difference between "moving on" and "moving forward?" How can your faith inform which is the healthiest?

3. Read Psalm 34:17-18. How can the promises of God help you walk through the grieving process?

A NEW HOPE

A pack can feel oppressively empty when someone who's guided, loved, and nurtured you passes away. We all felt that sadness when we lost Cole. He loved his young friend, and that love was instrumental in Franklin's transformation from frightened rescue pup to the loving dog who now visited Gina's parents without his best friend and teacher.

The home had never been without a dog. As Gina grew up in that house, there was an overlapping history of canine friends. Before Cole, there was Lady. Before Lady, there was a large Alaskan Malamute named King. Though Franklin visited often, the passing months revealed the need for another dog's joyful spirit to roam their halls again. Gina's family had always loved large dogs, but Franklin had melted their hearts for smaller rescue dogs.

As people leave our lives, God places new relationships in front of us. And the things we've learned about living a life of freedom affects how we see and react to those new people. Sometimes God puts new mentors in our lives, but

He'll often entrust us to become teachers to new friends who haven't discovered that same freedom.

Bella was tiny and neglected. She was half Franklin's size and shook continually. Her scrawny frame was weak and moved with uncertainty as she walked. We didn't think it possible, but she was in worse condition than Franklin had been when we'd rescued him years before. After a careful introduction, the two dogs quickly became friends, but Bella was timid and struggled with the most basic activities.

She had no interest in her new food dish. We placed her shivering body down in front of it, but she just stared forward. There was no expression on her face, just a blank effort to remain standing. She didn't know how to eat from a food dish.

"Let's let Franklin eat," someone said, moving Bella to the side. Franklin swept in and gobbled the food down like he'd never eaten before. He always found someone else's food more appetizing than his own.

At first, Gina's parents had to feed Bella by hand, but she continued to watch Franklin eat when he came to visit. She'd stand near the bowl and study Franklin as he ate. Finally, when Franklin trotted off from a well-loved meal one day, Bella came behind him with timid steps to check the dish. That was the beginning of her restoration. Week by week, she learned how to eat by following Franklin's example. Now, in the legacy of Cole's guidance, Franklin was to be Bella's mentor.

Eating wasn't Bella's only problem. Unlike Franklin, who immediately took to the game of fetch, Bella didn't seem to understand how to play. She didn't toss toys around, run, or explore. When she went outside, she'd go to the bathroom and then stand motionless, waiting for someone to come get her. Her trauma had erased every instinct but the one to exist. And her abuse had robbed any desire for her to seek joy or love.

But Franklin couldn't have this.

Each time they'd go into the yard together, Franklin performed a circus act of figure eight maneuvers, running with the intensity of a gazelle and the joy of a leaping fawn. He stopped right in front of her, challenging Bella to join him with a series of playful false starts. No response.

He darted off for another lap along the edge of the fence and skidded to a stop in front of her again. He crouched in a mocked stalking position with his tail wagging back and forth with excited purpose. There was a long pause as they looked at each other. Finally, and without warning, Bella shot off along the fence, and Franklin took chase. It only lasted for a few moments, but Franklin had broken through her hopelessness.

She soon learned how to jump into laps for companionship, and it wasn't long before Franklin and Bella were in friendly, if not awkward, competition for Pépère's leg space on the recliner.

The purpose of all these lessons we've explored is not only to make us better, but to equip us to reach out to those who are still broken. The final lesson Jesus gave us before ascending into Heaven was this:

> I have been given all authority in heaven and on earth. Therefore, go and make disciples of all the nations, baptizing them in the name of the Father and the Son and the Holy Spirit. Teach these new disciples to obey all the commands I have given you. And be sure

of this: I am with you always, even to the end of the age.

Matthew 28:18b–20 NLT

Just as Bella can trace her hope through the training pedigree of King, Lady, Cole, and Franklin, we can trace our spiritual lineage through those who invested in us when we were still hurting. Dogs were created to serve a purpose greater than themselves, and they're trained to fulfill that purpose. We misunderstand the meaning of Christianity when we believe the purpose of our freedom and discipleship is to meet our own needs. God designs our growth in a relationship with Him to reach those who are still huddled in the world's shelter, uncertain of their future. The only time our Christian lives should be about us is when we need more training or healing to better serve others.

When Paul wrote to Timothy, he started his letter by saying, "I am writing to Timothy, my true son in the faith. May God the Father and Christ Jesus our Lord give you grace, mercy, and peace" (1 Timothy 1:2 NLT). Who are your spiritual children? Who are you sharing the grace, mercy, and peace you've inherited with today?

Key Words

Discipleship, Great Commission, Hope.

CHEW ON THIS: QUESTIONS FOR YOU AND YOUR PACK TO GNAW ON

Reflect on the phrases or concepts that stood out to you in this chapter.

1. Read 1 Corinthians 9:19-22. How do you think this relates to your outreach and discipleship of others?

2. What is the difference between being in the culture and being influenced by the culture?

3. What would it take for you to share the same desperation for reaching others that Paul shows?

4. Spend time asking God who He wants you to invest in. What are some steps you can take in that direction?

COMING HOME

Just as Cole passed his legacy of compassion on through Franklin, one day we'll all slip into eternity and others will carry forward what God has done in their lives through us. Whatever pain we endure in this world will be washed away by the glory of our eternity. There may be times when we feel alone here, but Christ has promised to bring us home. Jesus said,

> Let not your hearts be troubled. Believe in God; believe also in me. In my Father's house are many rooms. If it were not so, would I have told you that I go to prepare a place for you? And if I go and prepare a place for you, I will come again and will take you to myself, that where I am you may be also.
>
> John 14:1-3 ESV

It's impossible to know what it will feel like that first moment we stand before Jesus. There's no illustration that can approach the reality of what we'll experience when we open our eyes in Paradise to see the glory of Jesus Christ. It's beyond imagination, but there is one daily event with Franklin that makes me ponder on that future encounter.

After a long day sitting with and encouraging people oppressed by a thousand cuts of hurt in this world, I pull into my driveway and stop my car. As the garage door slowly travels upward, a calmness comes over me because my favorite moment of the day is about to happen. I pull into the garage, grab my messenger bag, and walk into the laundry room. There's a commotion behind the door, and I experience a moment of joy. As the door opens into the kitchen, my eyes meet Franklin's from his large crate. He spins and jumps up to extend his gumdrop nose over the edge of the open-topped pen. He hops up and down on his hind legs, the excitement on his face undeniable.

"Hey, buddy," I say with a smile.

My voice only excites him more as he waves his front paws in unison while his hind legs continue bouncing. I open the gate, and he runs onto the kitchen floor, sliding as he catches his balance. As I bend down, he scrambles into my arms. He wriggles with happiness as I pick him up and kiss him on the head. Franklin is finally in the embrace of the one who truly loves him.

When I think about how many struggles Franklin faced in life to reach that moment of joy, I wonder what it will be like when I finish walking through this life and see the outstretched arms of Christ.

I am a rescue pup.

I've wandered through this world without a home, covered by the spiritual mange of sin. I've experienced cruelty at the hands of others. I've found myself infested with the parasite of lies Satan told me about who I am, sucking away my identity and hope. I've wondered how I would survive and questioned whether it was worth trying. I've experienced the false realization that I'm unwanted and unloved—that I am, in fact, unlovable.

I had heard these words for years:

> For God so loved the world that he gave his one and only Son, that whoever believes in him shall not perish but have eternal life. For God did not send his Son into the world to condemn the world, but to save the world through him.
>
> John 3:16-17 NIV

I knew the words, but until I began trusting that love, I could not experience it. God was calling my name, but I kept myself in a cold, dark kennel of anxiety and fear. I thought I only deserved the condemnation of Christ, not the life He came to offer.

The most important step in unleashing our soul is recognizing our leash is held by the world, a world that offers pain and a sorrow designed to convince us no one is coming to our rescue. But once I allowed myself to experience the love of God that I'd heard about so many times, I could live a life knowing I would inherit His final promise, "He will wipe every tear from their eyes. There will be no more death' or mourning or crying or pain, for the old order of things has passed away" (Revelation 21:4 NIV).

The first miracle of Franklin's life is that he lived, but the greatest is that he's loved. And that can be the greatest miracle of *our* lives when we're adopted by a Father who sent His Son to rescue a broken and abused people from the puppy mill of isolation, sin, and shame. We are loved not because we've overcome our past, but because of Christ's sacrifice to bring us home.

Key Themes

Eternity, Home, Salvation

CHEW ON THIS: QUESTIONS FOR YOU AND YOUR PACK TO GNAW ON

Reflect on the phrases or concepts that stood out to you in this chapter.

1. What is preventing you from fully experiencing the love of God?

2. Read Romans 8:38-39. How does this affect your view of eternity?

3. Read Romans 10:9-10. What is meant by the word "Lord" in this verse?

4. Are you willing to take or renew the steps described in Romans 10? If so, share your experience with someone else.

ACTION STEPS FOR AN UNLEASHED SOUL

Franklin's story is one of hope and restoration, but his journey from isolated brokenness to joyful belonging is only a dim reflection of the greater story God wants to write in your life.

Use the following action steps drawn from each of the thirty chapters to grow your faith and deepen your relationship with Christ. Learning to quiet our thoughts long enough to hear God takes time, so don't get frustrated. Use the personal reflection questions at the end of each chapter and prepare for the more difficult action steps during a daily time of silence.

1. Ask God to reveal how He sees you and your circumstances.

2. Meditate on God's desire to have you in His family.

3. Examine what worries you and write them down. Then write a short prayer under your list offering those worries to God.

4. Ask God to reveal what aspects of your past you've been hiding and how He wants to help clean it out.

5. Ask God what's been preventing you from accepting a greater portion of the abundant life He offers.

6. Using an internet search engine, look up and reflect on Scriptures describing your identity in Christ (start with Ephesians 1:4-6; Romans 8:39).

7. Discuss your past and current scars with God and another believer you can trust.

8. List the things you view as restrictions in your life and ask God how they're meant to protect you.

9. Take an inventory of your relationships, evaluating which ones help draw you closer to God and which ones lead you farther away from Him. Get connected to a healthy group of Christians.

10. Reach out to an individual whose faith can be an encouragement to you as you grow.

11. Ask God to reveal how He's uniquely gifted you to serve Him and others.

12. Be intentional in looking for opportunities to be present with people who are hurting.

13. Set a daily time to be present with God, read the Bible, and silently rest as you reflect on His Word.

14. Practice waiting for God to act on your behalf with patience and trust. Write down the things you're waiting for and ask God two questions: "Is this thing I'm waiting for good for me?" and "What do You want me to do while I wait?"

15. Ask God to show you the areas in your life where you're trying to disassemble what He's putting in place for you.

16. Remind yourself that joy is God's desire for you. Find a few moments to experience joy every day.

17. Reflect on the seemingly impossible things God has done in someone else's life. Ask what He's preparing you to do in His kingdom and how you can surrender your fear.

18. Find someone who's struggling with their faith and offer to walk through the healing process with them.

19. Ask God to teach you what He needs you to know in order to better serve Him with purpose.

20. Remove people, places, and items of temptation from your life.

21. Ask God to reveal how you're using the gifts He's given you for selfish gain.

22. Practice trusting in God's provision and gifts by evaluating the things you want (or refuse to let go of) and asking God what He wants to give you.

23. List the things that cause anxiety or create uncontrolled emotions in your life. Pray for God's touch in each area you identified.

24. Surrender control of anything or anyone God has not given you direct authority over. Evaluate how you

approach the people and things He *has* given you authority over.

25. Sit silently on a regular basis, expecting an experience with God. Ask Him to show you how He best speaks to you.

26. When you find it difficult to calm yourself to hear God in crisis, reflect on the experiences you've had practicing the last action step.

27. Practice telling God how you really feel. Have an honest and transparent conversation with Him about your struggles, fear, and pain.

28. Ask God to show you any loss you haven't fully grieved (e.g. a person, job, or dream). Explore healthy ways to honor that grief.

29. Invest in the life of someone who does not share your faith in Christ. Be an encouragement and servant to them.

30. Reflect on the glory of Christ and His willingness to rescue us. Ask Him to guide you in accepting the new life He offers or in rededicating your life to fulfill His greater purpose for you in His family.

INDEX OF
KEY THEMES

ABOUT JOSHUA J. MASTERS

Joshua J. Masters is a pastor, author, and speaker with a heart for encouraging others as they pursue a deeper relationship with Christ. His book, American Psalms, a Serious Writer's Book of the Decade finalist, teaches readers how to pray for America by seeking God rather than political outcomes.

Josh has been featured on CBN Television, HIS Radio, the Light Radio Network, and is a regular teacher and speaker for large groups. As a member of the Screen Actors Guild (SAG-AFTRA), he's also worked in the stage, film, and television industries. Maintaining his love for movies and all things creative, Josh is a self-proclaimed sci-fi and comic book geek. His not-so-secret alter ego, the Bat Pastor, loves sharing the gospel through the parables of pop-culture.

In his monthly column for the award-winning website, The Write Conversation, Josh shares spiritual advice and encouragement to other writers. He's been published in Refresh Bible Study Magazine, One Christian Voice, and was a contributing author for the Selah Awards finalist, Feed Your Soul with the Word of God. As an advocate for faith-based recovery, Josh has taught at an international event for Bridge Builders, worked as a Celebrate Recovery pastor, and served on the Vermont governors' panel to combat opiate addiction.

Raised in the White Mountains of New England, Joshua is now a pastor in South Carolina where he lives and serves with his wife, Gina. Together, they love going on adventures with their miniature poodle, Franklin the Pup. Josh would love to connect with you on his website, JoshuaJMasters. com.

ABOUT FRANKLIN

Franklin P. Masters is a pastor's pup, avid barker, and an imagination-based writer like his favorite canine protagonist, Snoopy. Sadly, the early days of Franklin's life could rival his hero's "dark and stormy night." Neglected and abused, Franklin was rescued from a cruel puppy mill by a rescue organization in New Hampshire, which led to his new life of hope with Joshua and Gina Masters.

Although he's not a fan of birds or doorbells, Franklin the Pup is loving with small children and has a discerning heart. He can always sense the gentle spirit of a kind visitor and quickly alerts his family if there's someone they shouldn't trust.

Franklin enjoys long runs on the beach, coffee cuddles, and playing fetch. And his passion for pizza crust, broccoli stalks, and "pupcorn" has led him to develop excellent tableside begging skills. His cuteness cannot be denied, and his button eyes and gumdrop nose won't hesitate to remind you of that when he wants something. From a place of utter rejection, Franklin is now dearly loved.

He would love to connect with you on his social media accounts available at www.FranklinThePup.com.